Days of our Lives

45 YEARS

A CELEBRATION IN PHOTOS

Like Sands Through the Hourglass...

GREG MENG AND EDDIE CAMPBELL

Published by Sourcebooks, Inc.
P.O. Box 4410, Naperville, Illinois 60567-4410
(630) 961-3900
Fax: (630) 961-2168
www.sourcebooks.com

CIP data is on file with the publisher.

Printed and bound in China.
OGP 10 9 8 7 6 5 4 3 2 1

"HORTON" LIVING ROOM SET (1965)

IN THE BEGINNING

CONTENTS

"TOM HORTON"/MACDONALD CAREY AND "ALICE HORTON"/FRANCES REID (1967)

6   "ADDIE OLSON"/PATRICIA BARRY READING HER LINES WITH CREW ON "HORTON" LIVING ROOM SET (1971)

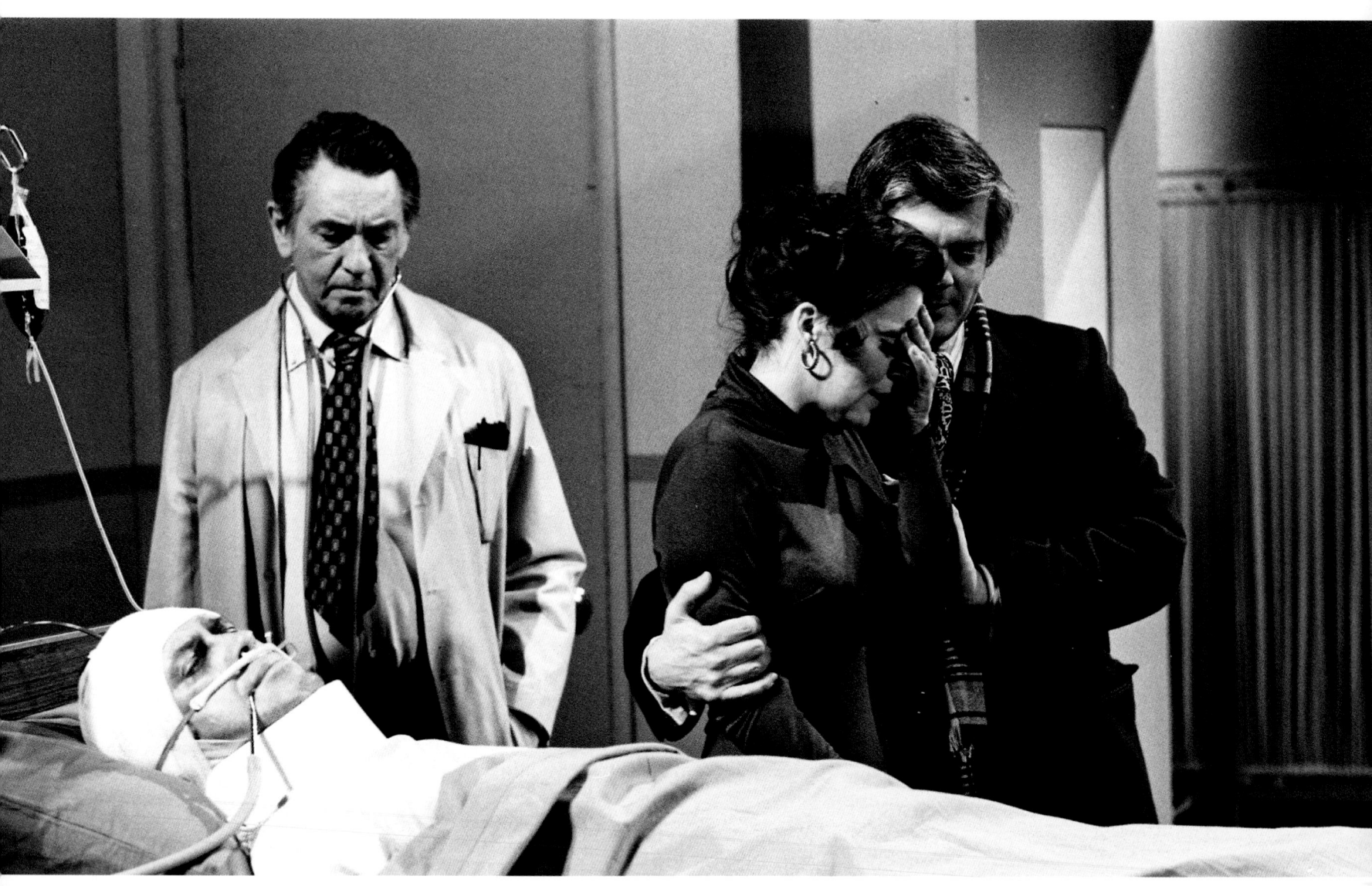

"SCOTT BANNING"/RYAN MACDONALD, "DR. TOM HORTON"/MACDONALD CAREY, "JULIE"/SUSAN SEAFORTH HAYES, AND "DOUG"/BILL HAYES—SCOTT (JULIE'S FIRST HUSBAND) DIES AFTER BEING HIT BY A FALLING BEAM (1973)

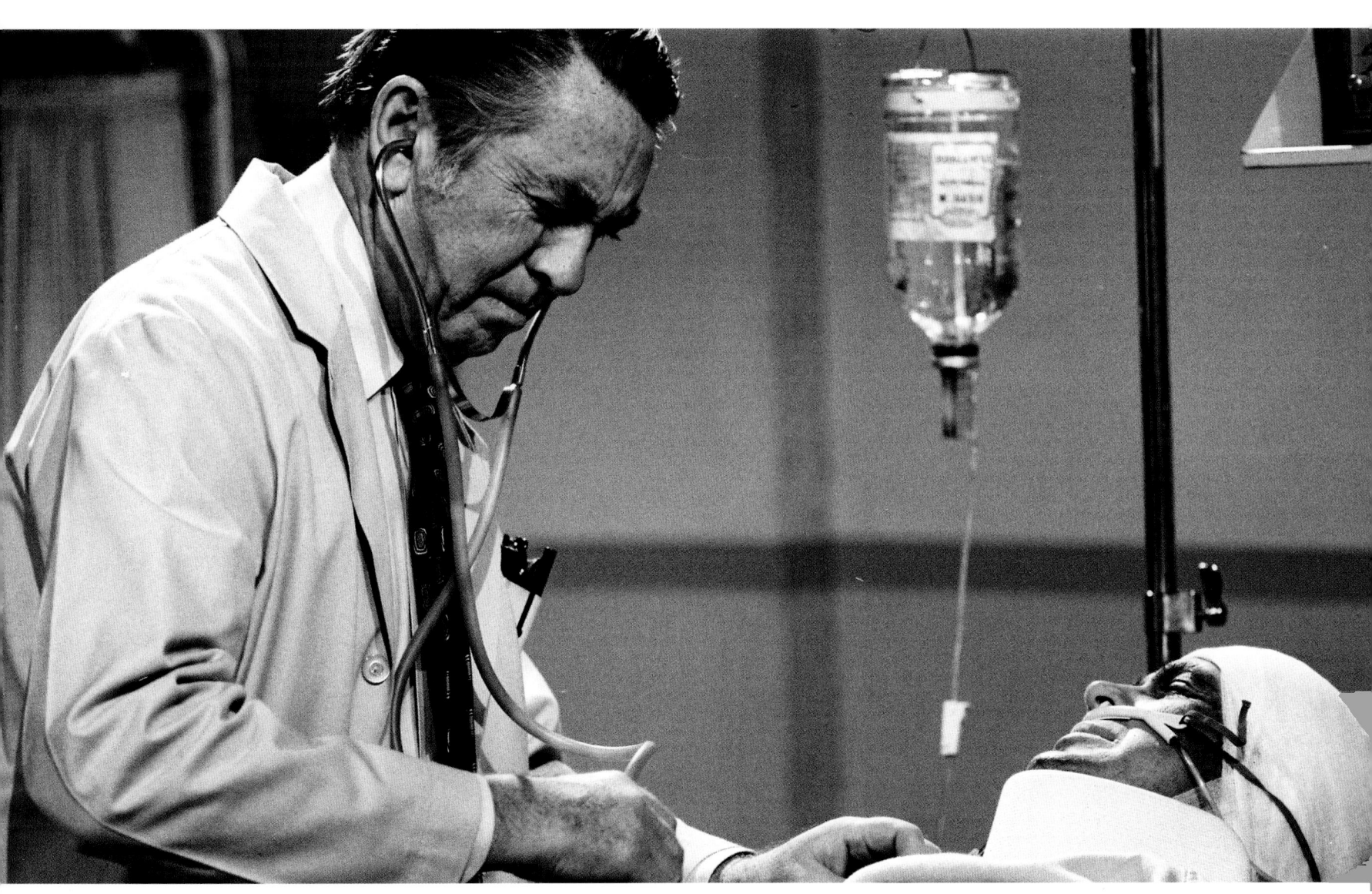

"ALICE"/FRANCES REID AND "JULIE"/SUSAN
SEAFORTH HAYES IN "HORTON"
LIVING ROOM (1969)

10

"MAGGIE"/SUZANNE ROGERS
AND UNKNOWN STYLIST IN
HAIR AND MAKEUP
(1974)

"JULIE"/SUSAN SEAFORTH HAYES
IN HAIR AND MAKEUP
(1974)

ABOVE: EXECUTIVE PRODUCER AND DIRECTOR/WES KENNEY AND "ANNE PETERS"/JEANNE BATES (1973)

LEFT: UNKNOWN MAN AND WES KENNEY (1974)

INTRODUCTION

This book is a celebration of *Days of our Lives*, beginning with never-before-seen vintage black-and-white and color photos, and culminating in a once-in-a-lifetime photographic journey of a day in the life of the show's taping. Also included are beautiful hand sketches of costumes that transformed Deidre Hall and other cast members into amazing works of living art. The book begins with early 1960s photos, continuing through the colorful '70s, and on through the fun and creative fashions of the '80s and '90s and into the new millennium and today. This book embraces the over four decades *Days* has been on television. Corday Productions is proud to present this unprecedented book, and dedicates it to the millions of fans worldwide who have made the show a historic success.

ABOVE: SEPARATE BEDS FOR COUPLES WERE INDICATIVE OF THE ERA (1965)

LEFT: "TOM AND ALICE" AT HOME (1967)

ABOVE: "DOUG"/BILL HAYES AND "JULIE"/SUSAN SEAFORTH HAYES REHEARSING LINES (1974)

RIGHT: "ROMAN"/JOSH TAYLOR AND "ABE"/JAMES REYNOLDS ON A LUNCH BREAK (2002)

"PATCH"/STEPHEN NICHOLS ON SET IN "EUROPE" (1986)

"BO"/PETER RECKELL (1990)

"BRADY"/KYLE LOWDER (2002)

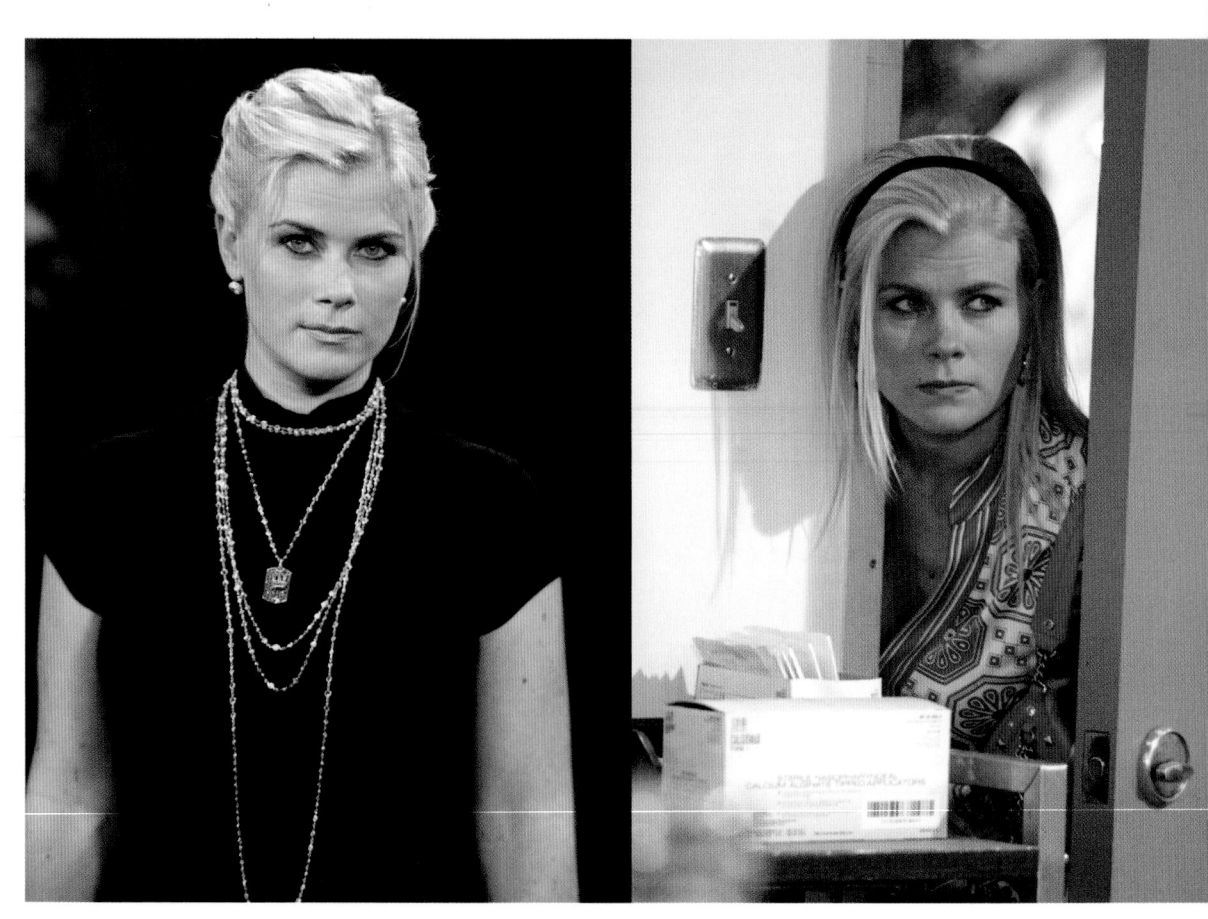

FACES OF "SAMI"/ALISON SWEENEY

ABOVE: "THE CRUISE OF DECEPTION" MASKED BALL, "GUINEVERE"/MELISSA REEVES & "KING ARTHUR"/
MATTHEW ASHFORD AND "PETRUCCHIO"/JOHN ANISTON & "KATE"/SUSAN SEAFORTH HAYES (1990)
LEFT PAGE TOP: "HOPE"/KRISTIAN ALFONSO AS "PRINCESS GINA" (1999)
LEFT PAGE BOTTOM: "SISTER COLLEEN"/ALISON SWEENEY (2007) AND "CALLIOPE"/ARLEEN SORKIN (1986)
BELOW: "JUDGE SHAY"/KEN CORDAY—EPISODE 10,000 (2005)

"BO"/PETER RECKELL AND "CARLY"/CRYSTAL CHAPPELL
(1992)

"BO" AND "HOPE"/KRISTIAN ALFONSO

ROMANCE

RIGHT TOP: "KAYLA"/MARY BETH EVANS AND "PATCH"/STEPHEN NICHOLS (1990)
LEFT TOP: "AUSTIN"/AUSTIN PECK AND "CARRIE"/CHRISTIE CLARK

RIGHT BOTTOM: "JENNIFER"/MELISSA REEVES AND "JACK"/MATTHEW ASHFORD
LEFT BOTTOM: "BO AND HOPE" (2005)

"DR. MARLENA EVANS"/DEIDRE HALL (1984)

"MARLENA" AND "JOHN"/DRAKE HOGESTYN (2002)

2006

2005

2005

1995

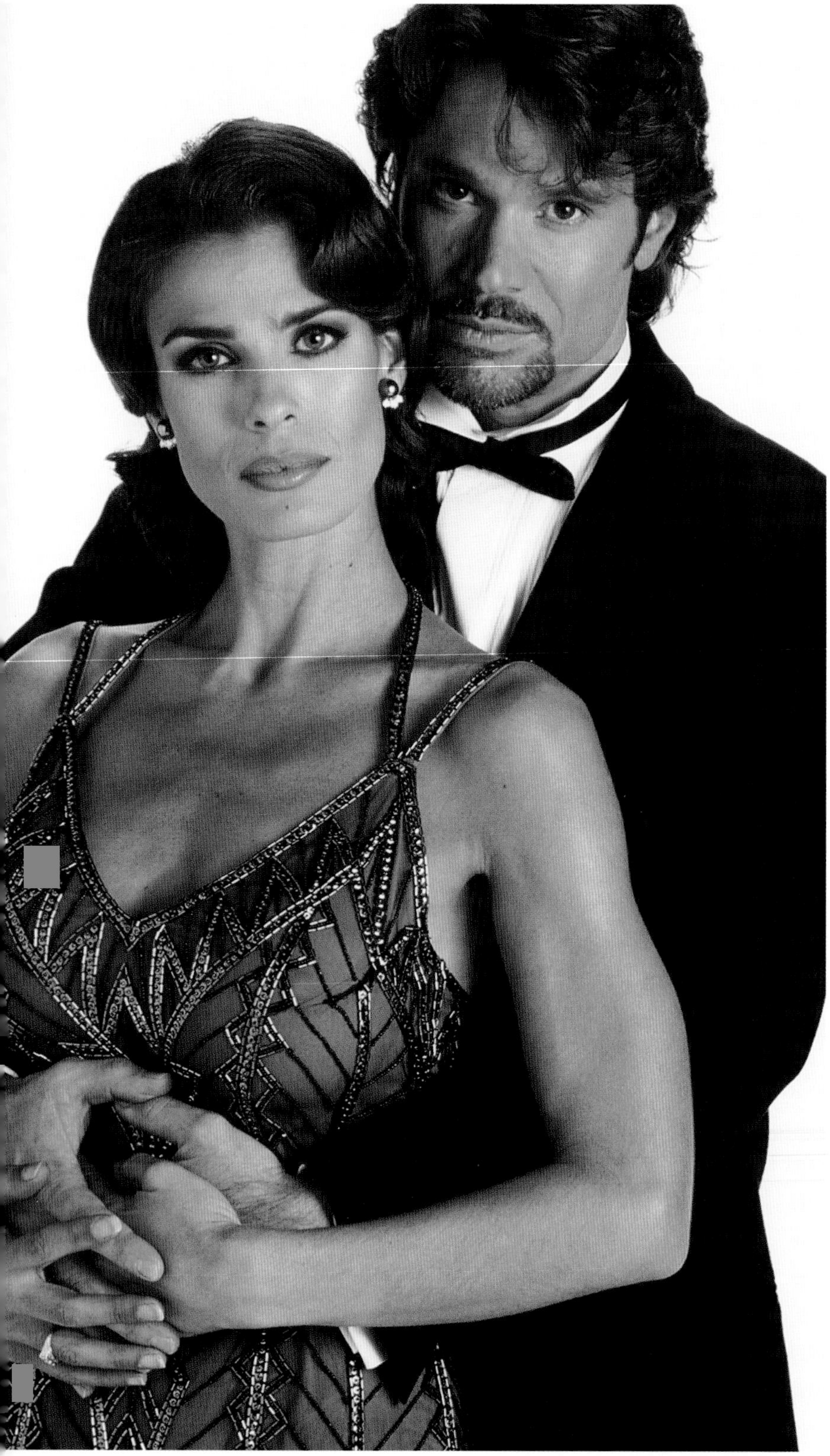

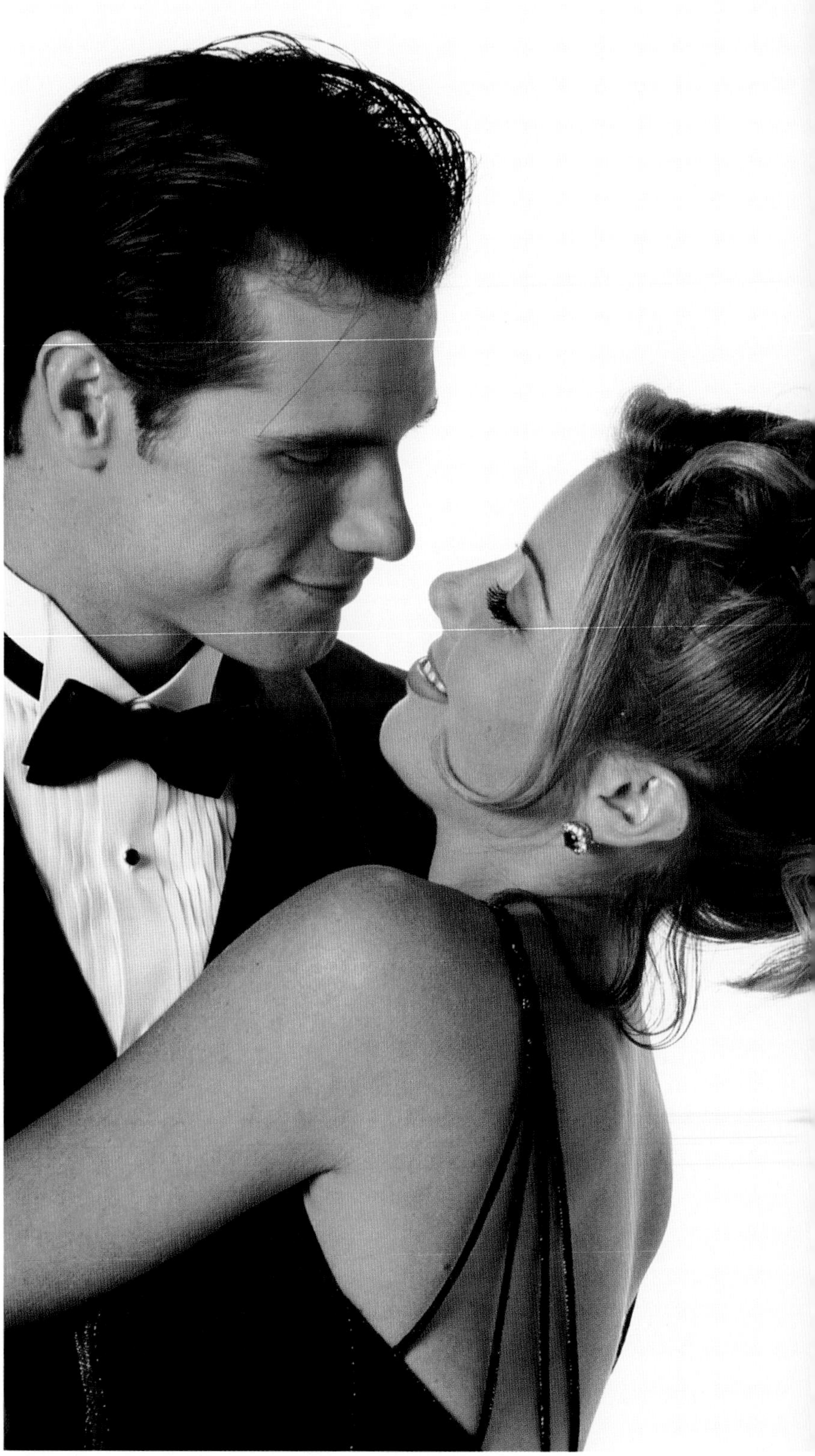

"BO" FEEDING WEDDING CAKE TO "HOPE" (1985)

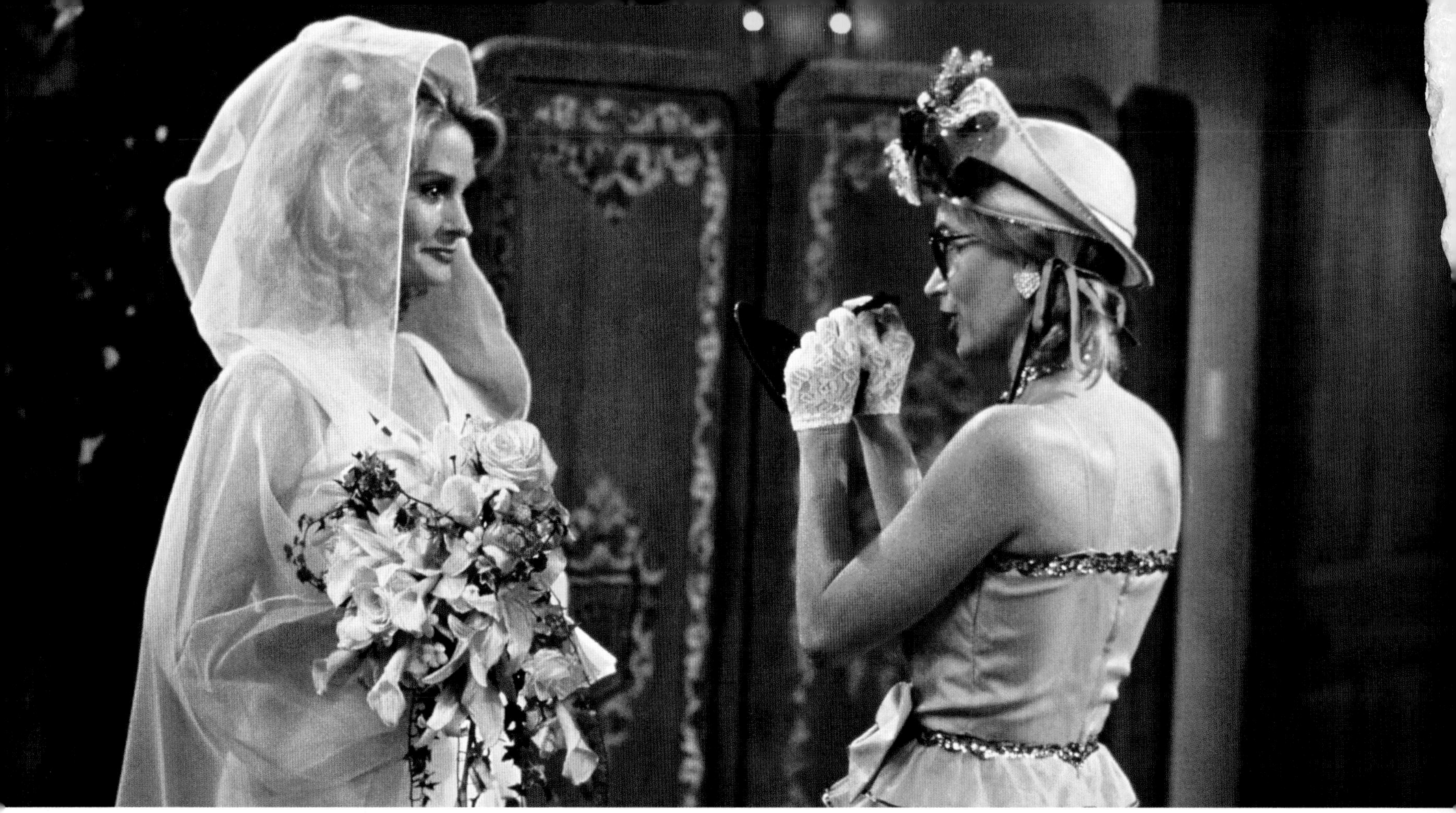

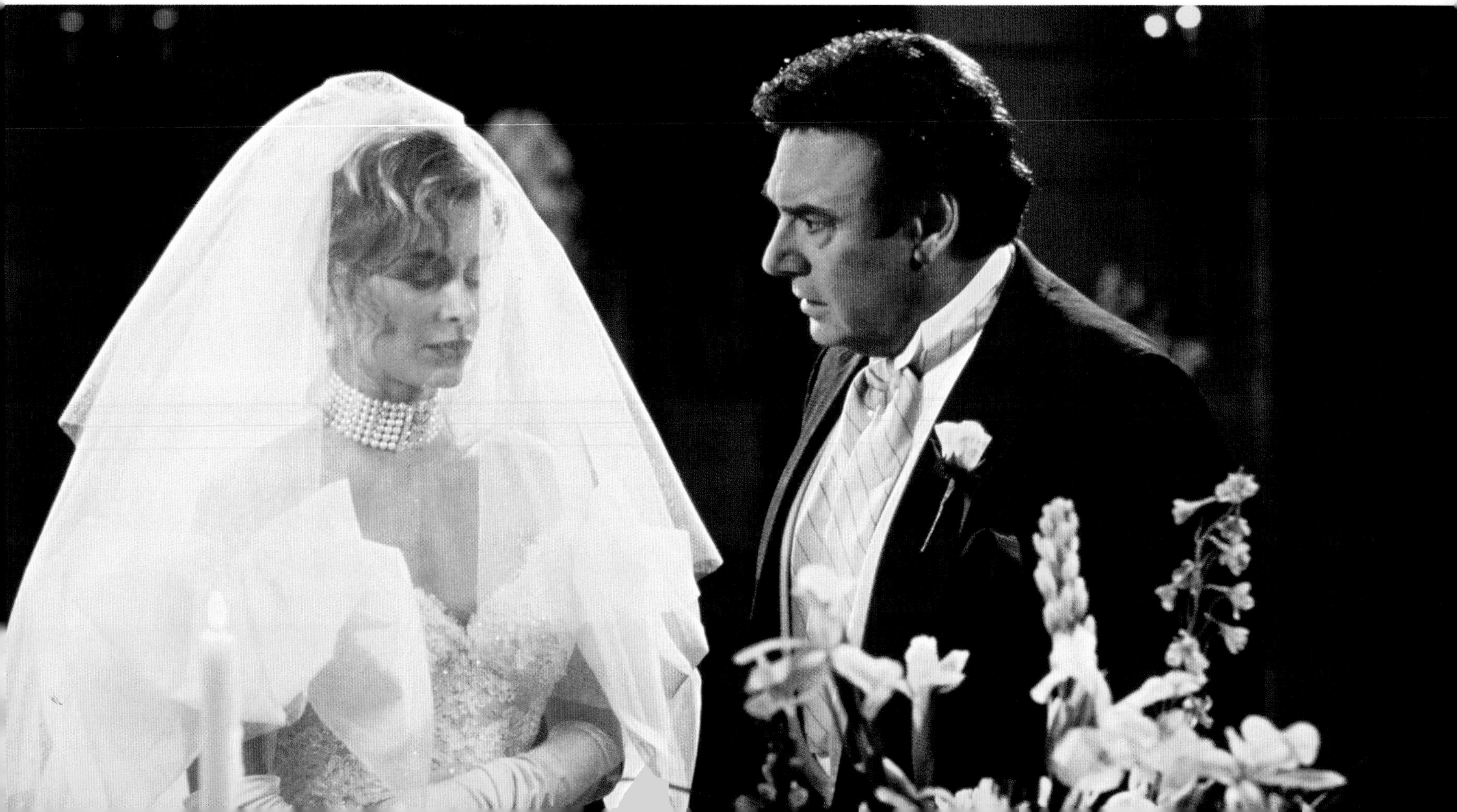

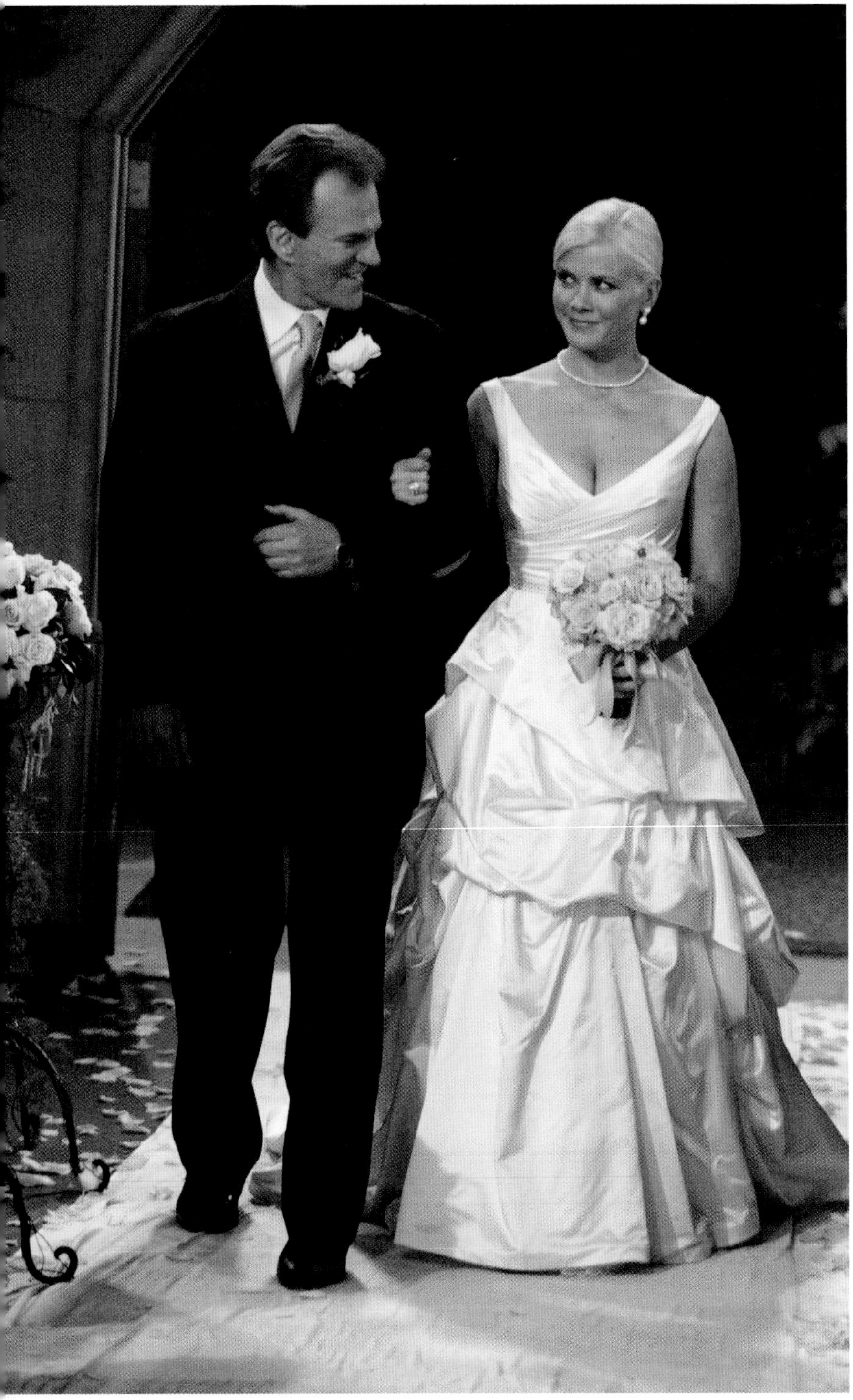

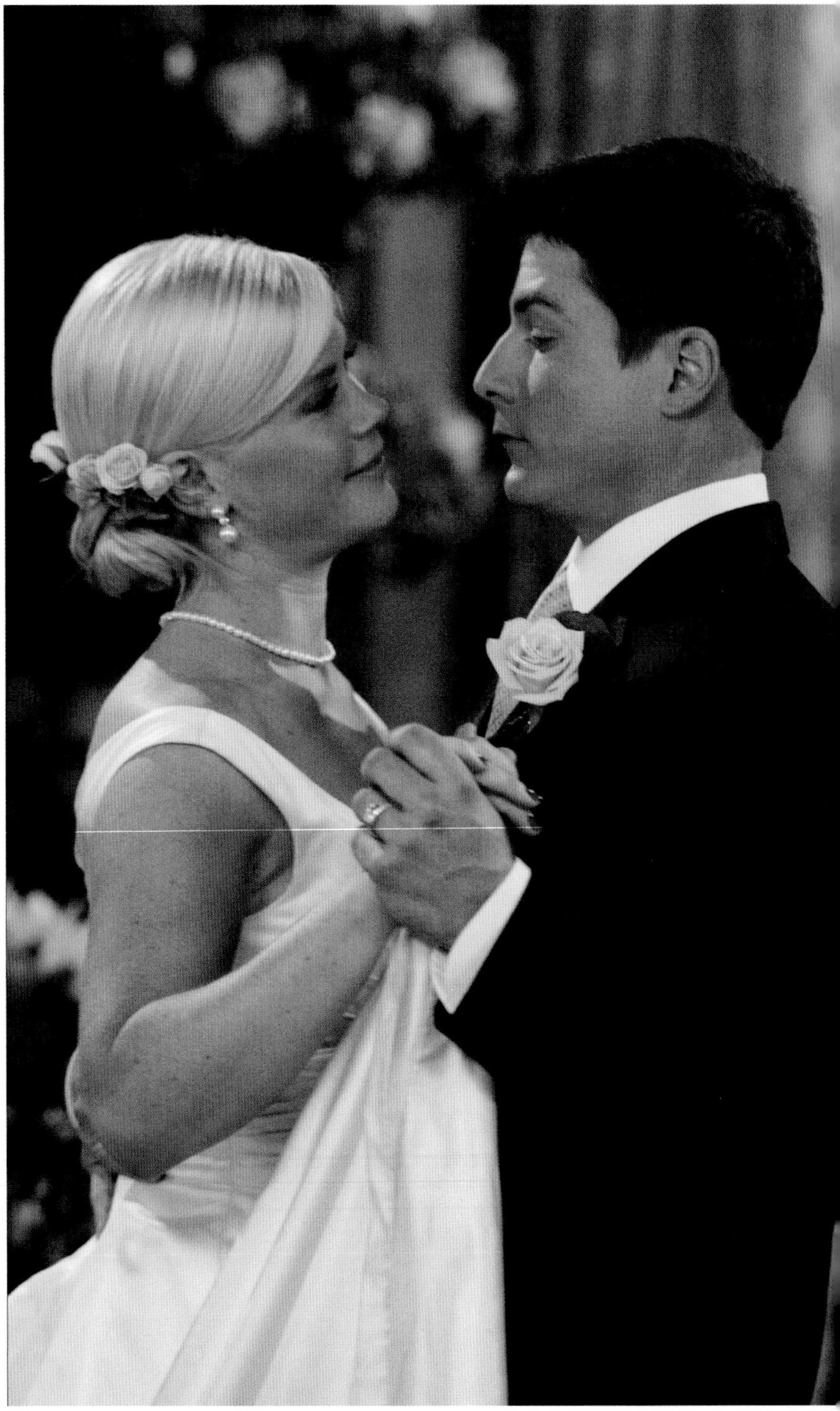

"SAMI"/ALISON SWEENEY, "ROMAN"/JOSH TAYLOR, AND "LUCAS"/BRYAN DATTILO—"THE GREEN WEDDING" (2007)

KRISTAN
WEDDING DRESS
OVER BEADED LACE
W/ ORGANZA TRAIN

VEIL IRRIDESENT NET

COSTUMES DESIGNED BY RICHARD BLOORE

KRISTAN
WEDDING DRESS
OVER BEADED LACE
W/ ORGANZA TRAIN

VEIL IRRIDESENT NET

BLOORE

CHIEFFON HOODED
OVER JACKET

SIMPLE
A-LINE
SHEATH
UNDER DRESS
4 PLY

MARLENA
WEDDING DRESS
& COAT

BLOORE

LEXIE GOWN
RED SATIN
w/ GOLD SATIN
LINING

DRAPE
CAN
A HOO

LEXIE GOWN
RED SATIN
w/ GOLD
LINING

MOORE

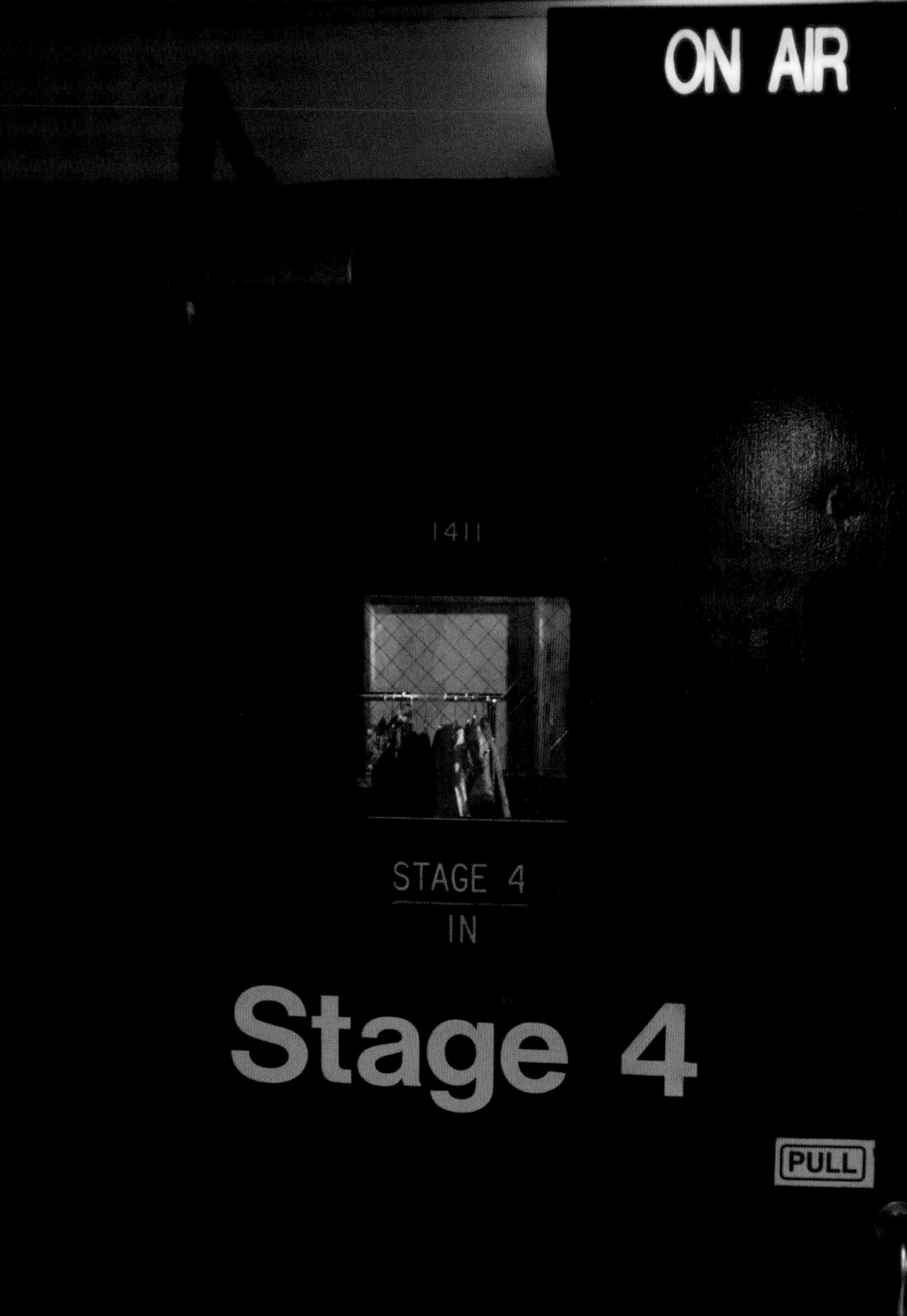

A DAY IN OUR LIFE

Days of our Lives is pleased to invite you on its very first tour of a day in the life of the show's taping. You will see the entire process up close and personally, including the early morning hours of hair and makeup, taping all day on set, and the final shot of the night. In addition, you will have intimate access to the cast's dressing rooms, which you can see only in this book, as well as a special feature on set plans, spectacular stage photos, and impromptu moments. In fact, for the first time in 45 years, you will even see the famous Horton Christmas tree ornaments. Family values are the core of *Days of our Lives*, and we welcome you as a part of our family to sit back and enjoy this truly special behind-the-scenes glimpse into our world. (2010)

RIGHT:
"HOPE"/KRISTIAN ALFONSO GUIDES YOU THROUGH THIS RARE PEEK INTO THE MAKING OF THE LONGEST-RUNNING DAYTIME DRAMA IN HISTORY.

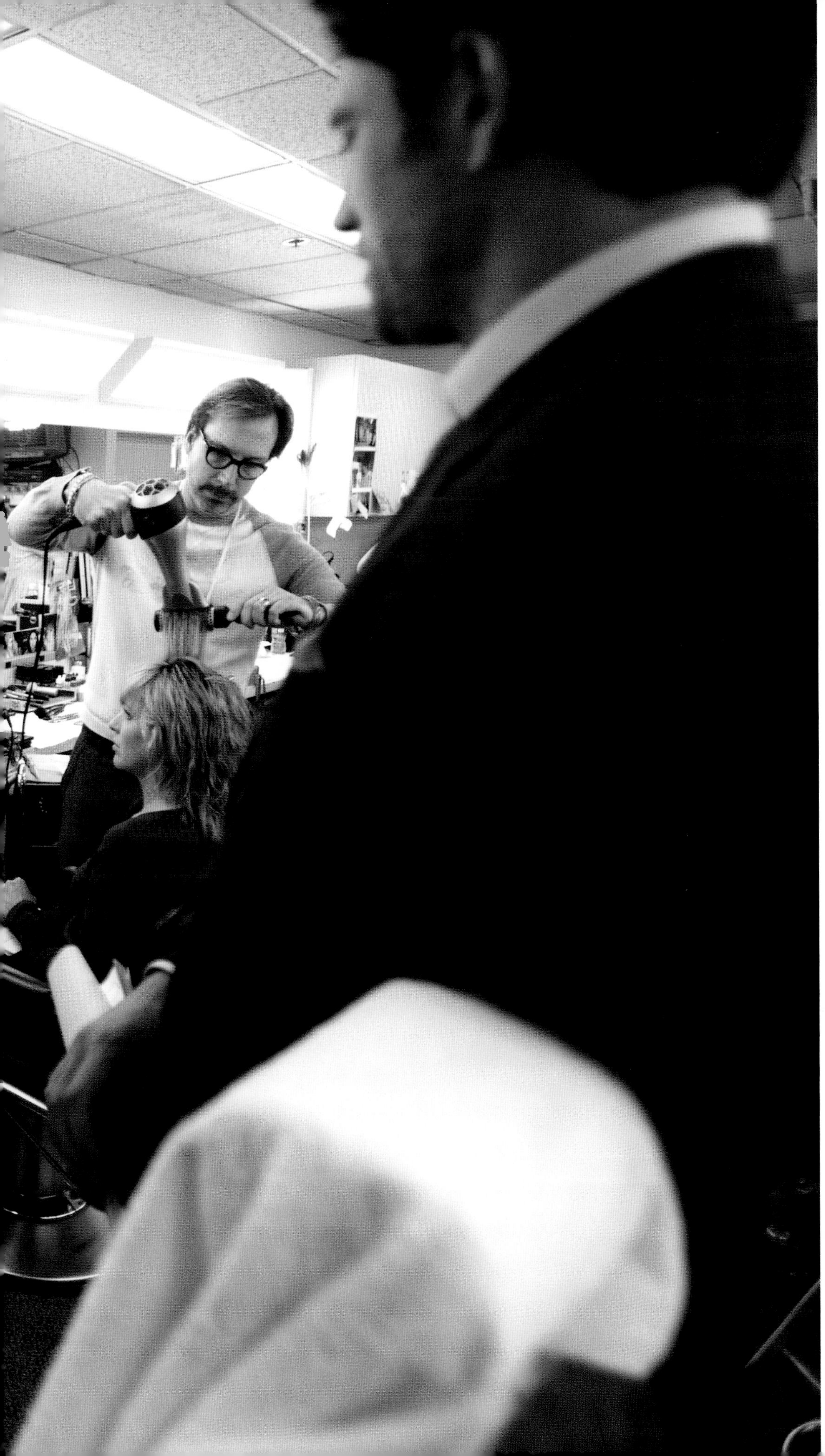

EARLY MORNING IN HAIR AND MAKEUP

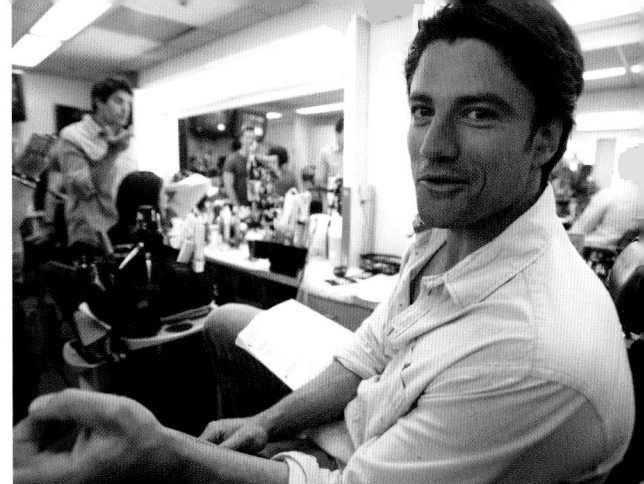

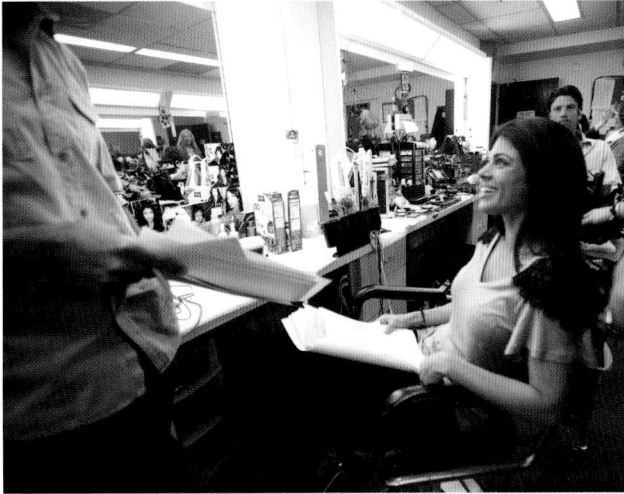

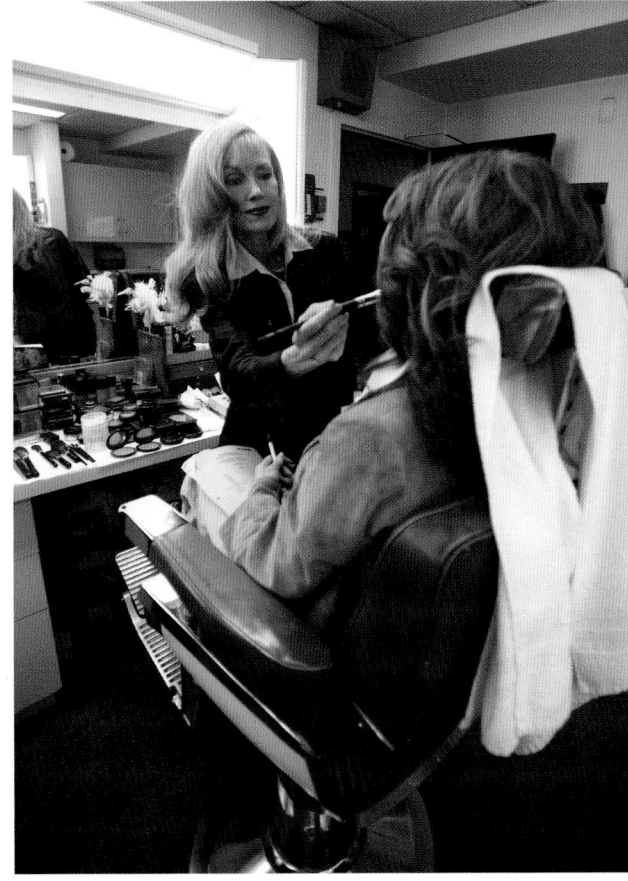

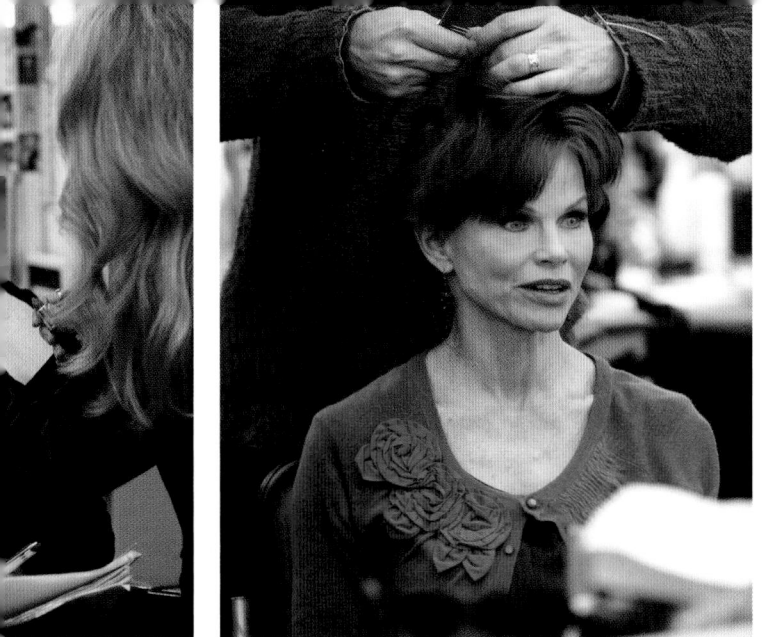

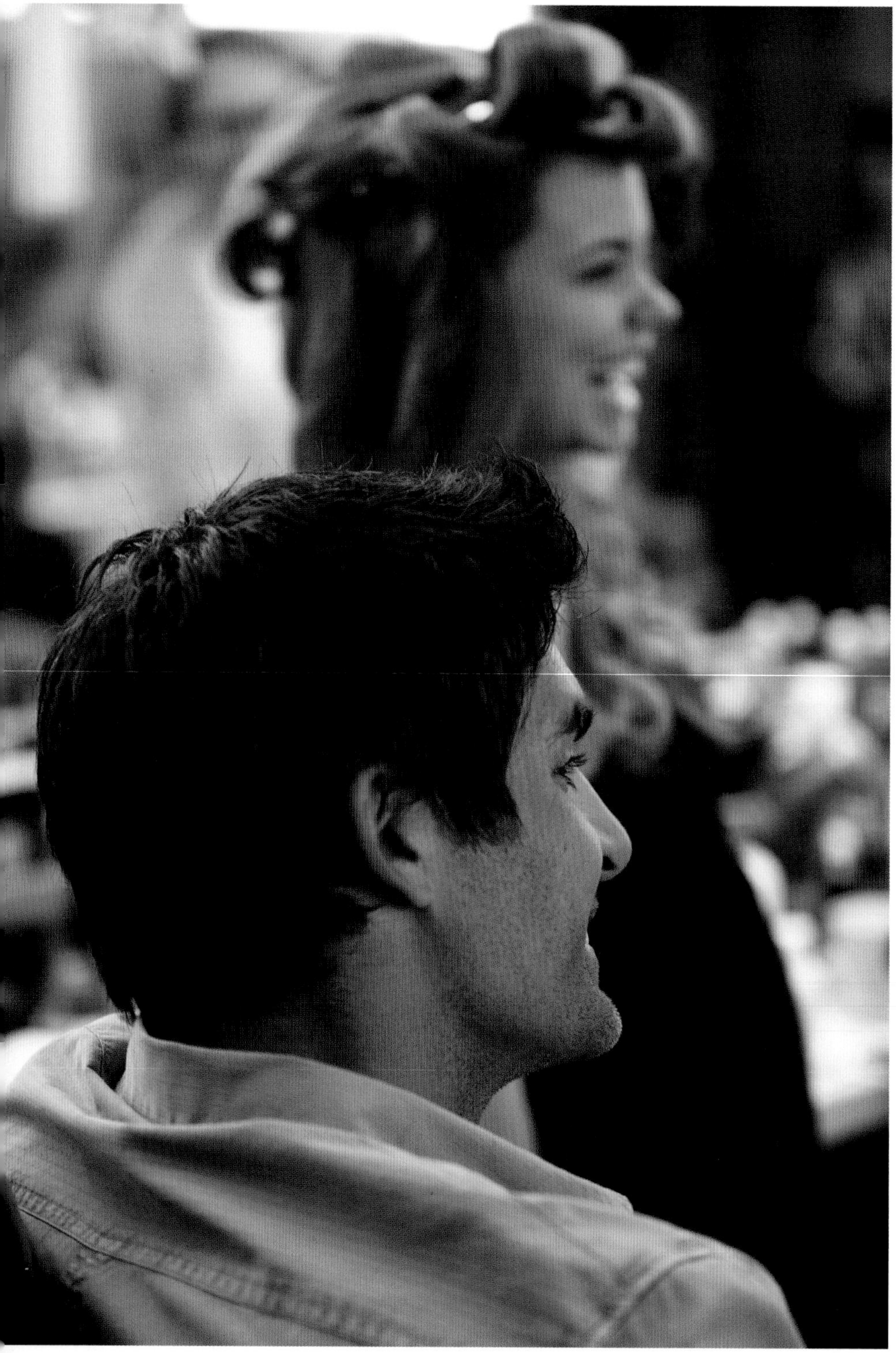

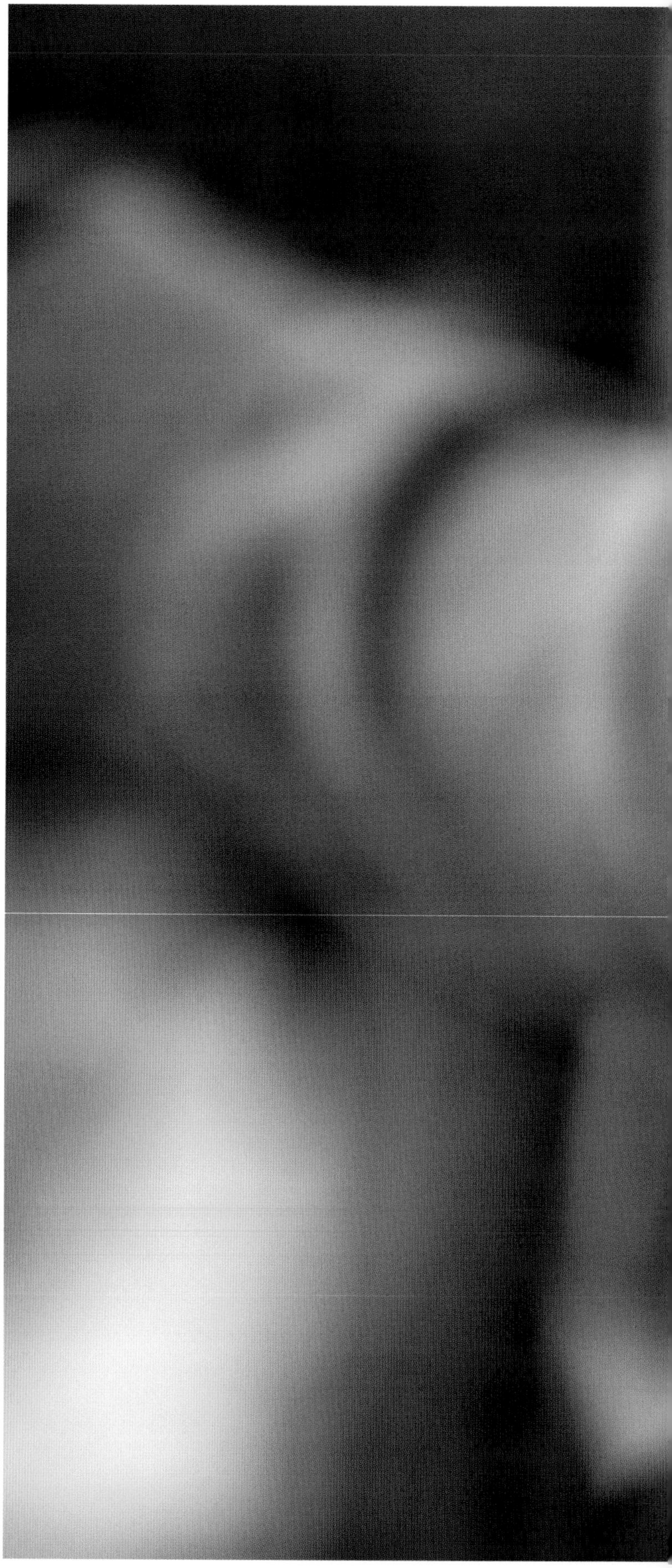

"LEXIE"/RENÉE JONES

"KATE"/LAUREN KOSLOW DOING A LAST-MINUTE TOUCH-UP

"LUCAS"/BRYAN DATTILO

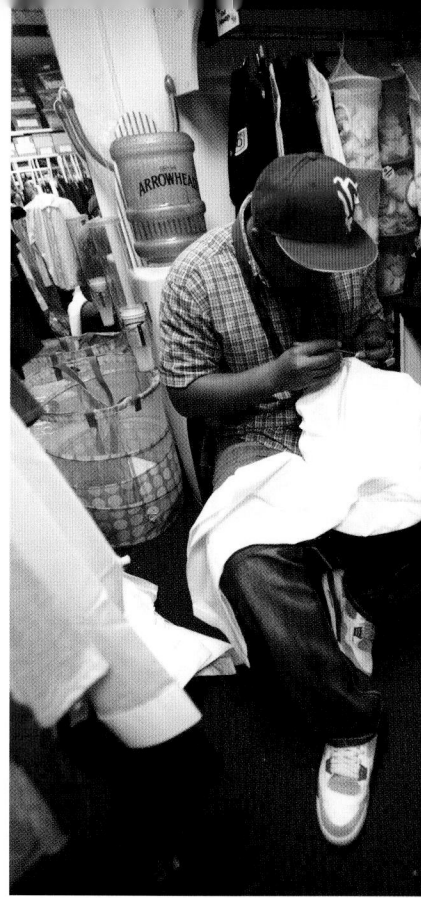

COSTUME DESIGNER/JAYNE KEHOE AND "HOPE"/KRISTIAN ALFONSO IN WARDROBE

WARDROBE HANDLER/
JAMMIE HARRIS

"CHAD"/CASEY JON DEIDRICK AND "RAFE"/GALEN GERING

JAYNE, KRISTIAN, AND WARDROBE HANDLER/DAISY SYLBERT-TORRES

"LEXIE"/RENÉE JONES IN WARDROBE

STUDIO 4
STUDIO 2

STUDIO
2
STUDIO
4

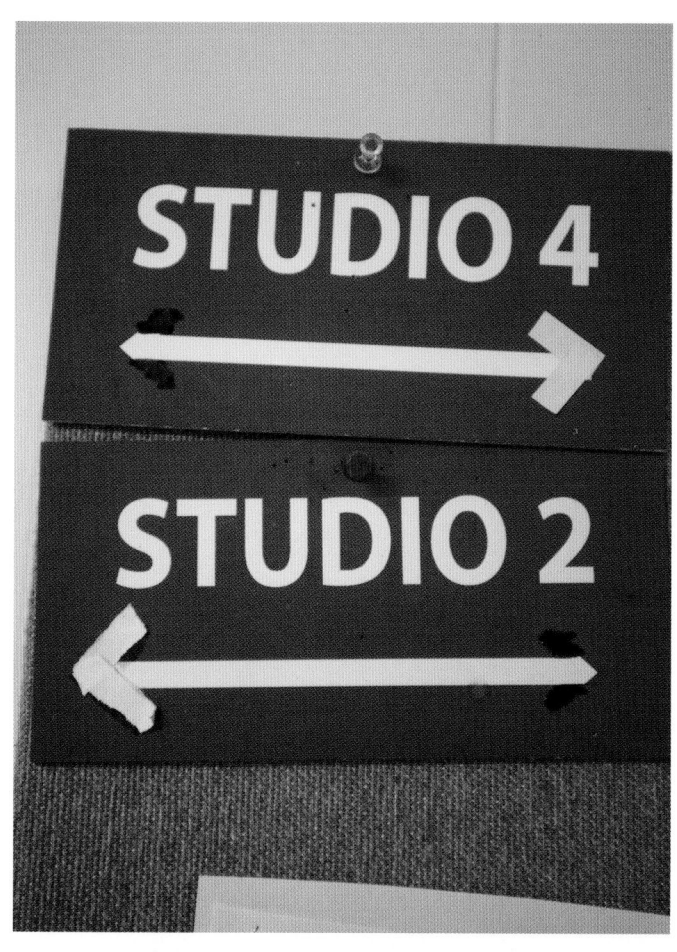

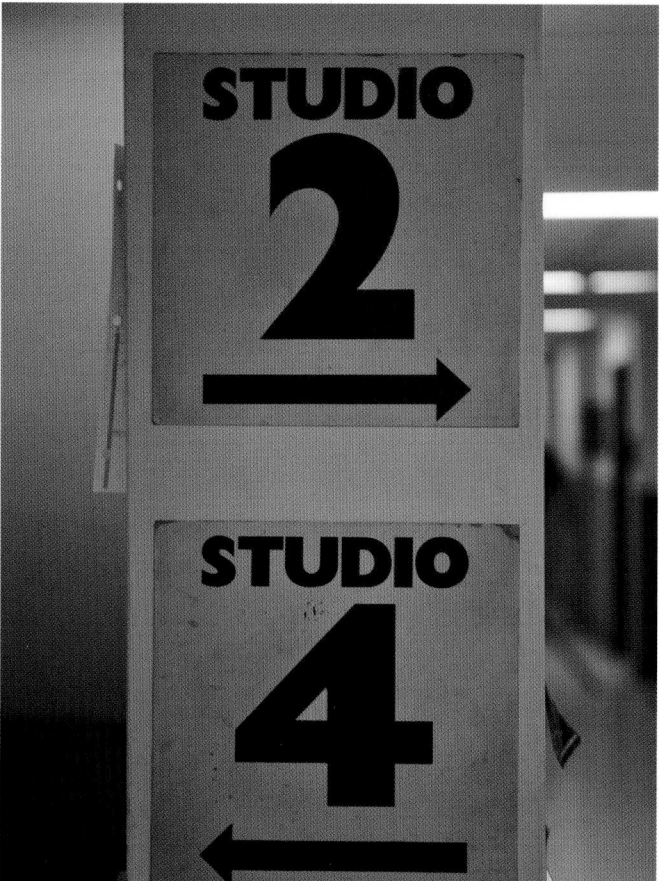

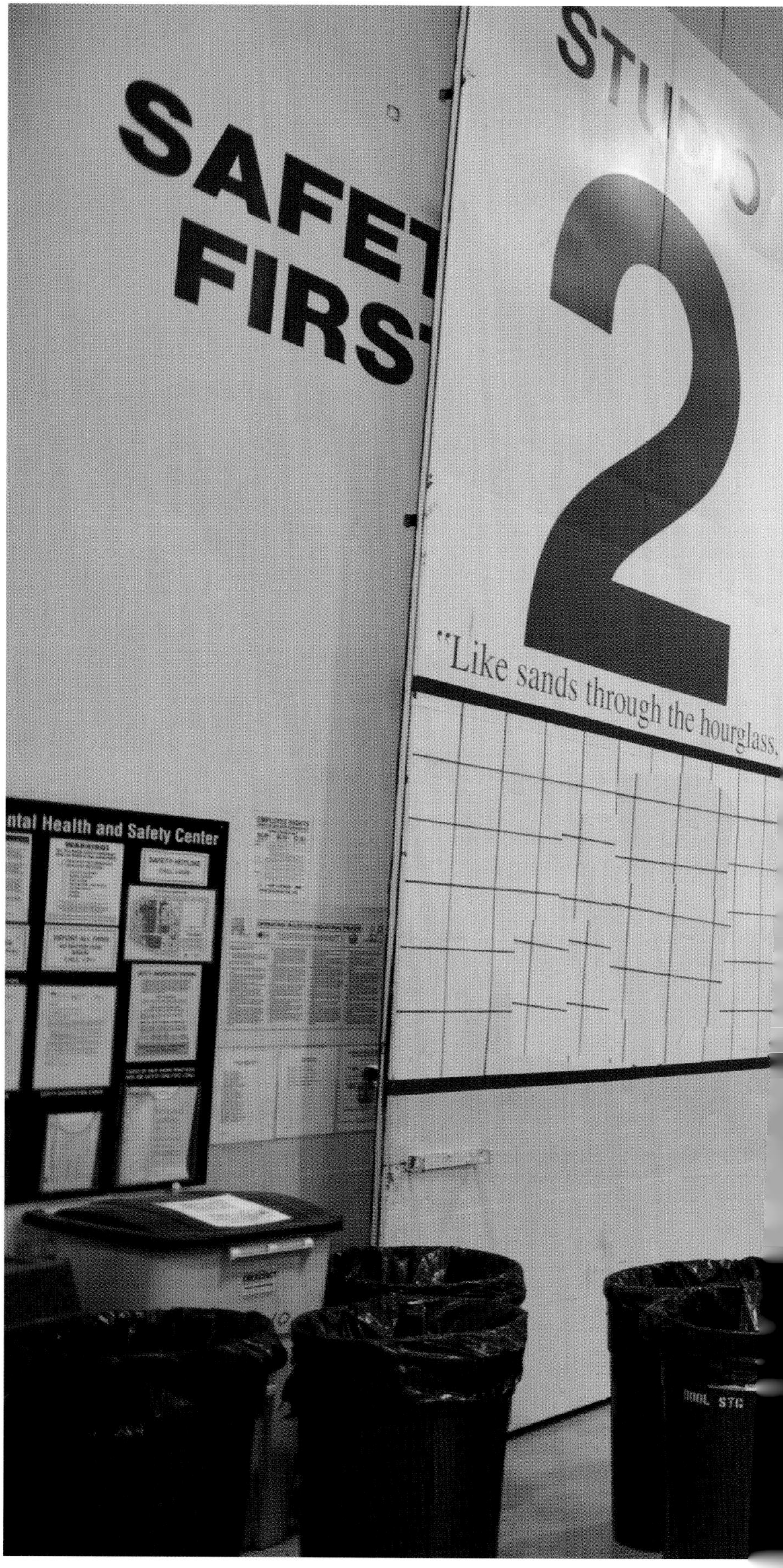
SAFET
FIRS
2
"Like sands through the hourglass,
ntal Health and Safety Center

FLOOR PROP HANDLER/MARIA QUINTANAR-HALL, PRODUCER/NOEL MAXAM, "RAFE"/GALEN GERING,

AND "SAMI"/ALISON SWEENEY IN THE "DIMERA" LIVING ROOM

"MELANIE"/MOLLY BURNETT BETWEEN SCENES

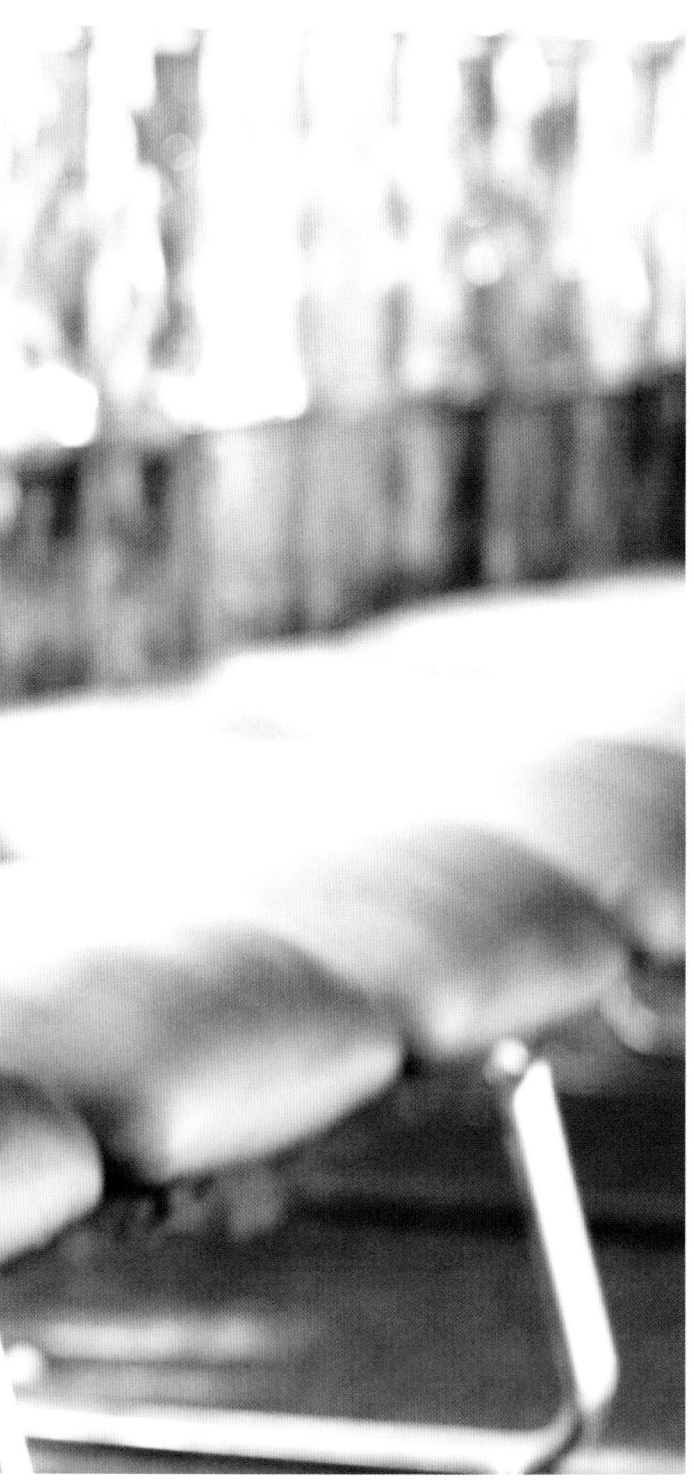

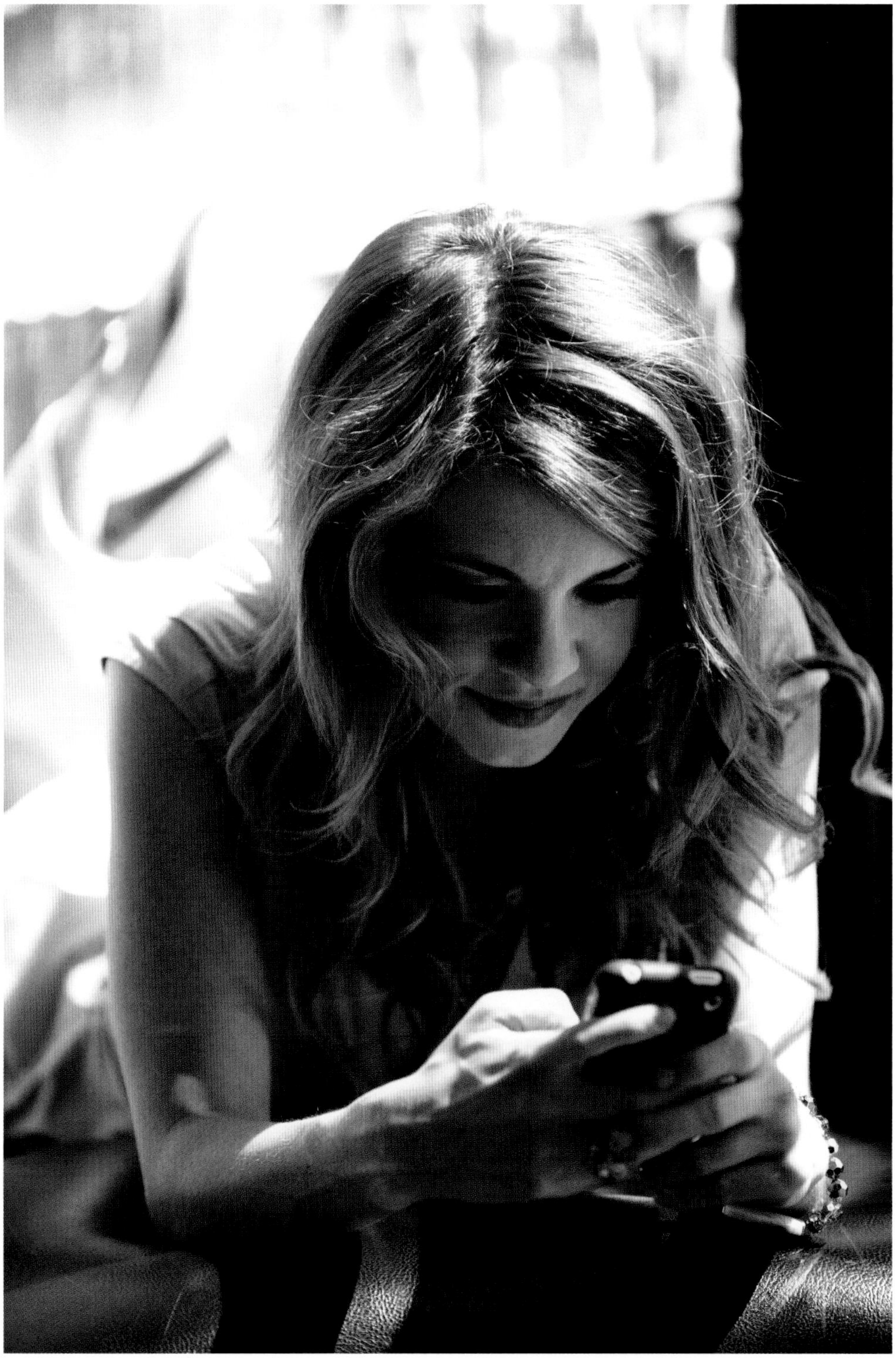

"ABE"/JAMES REYNOLDS GETTING INTO CHARACTER

"MAGGIE"/SUZANNE ROGERS
ON "HORTON" LIVING ROOM SET

"MELANIE"/MOLLY BURNETT, "PHILIP"/JAY
JOHNSON, AND "CHLOE"/NADIA BJORLIN
REHEARSING IN MOLLY'S DRESSING ROOM

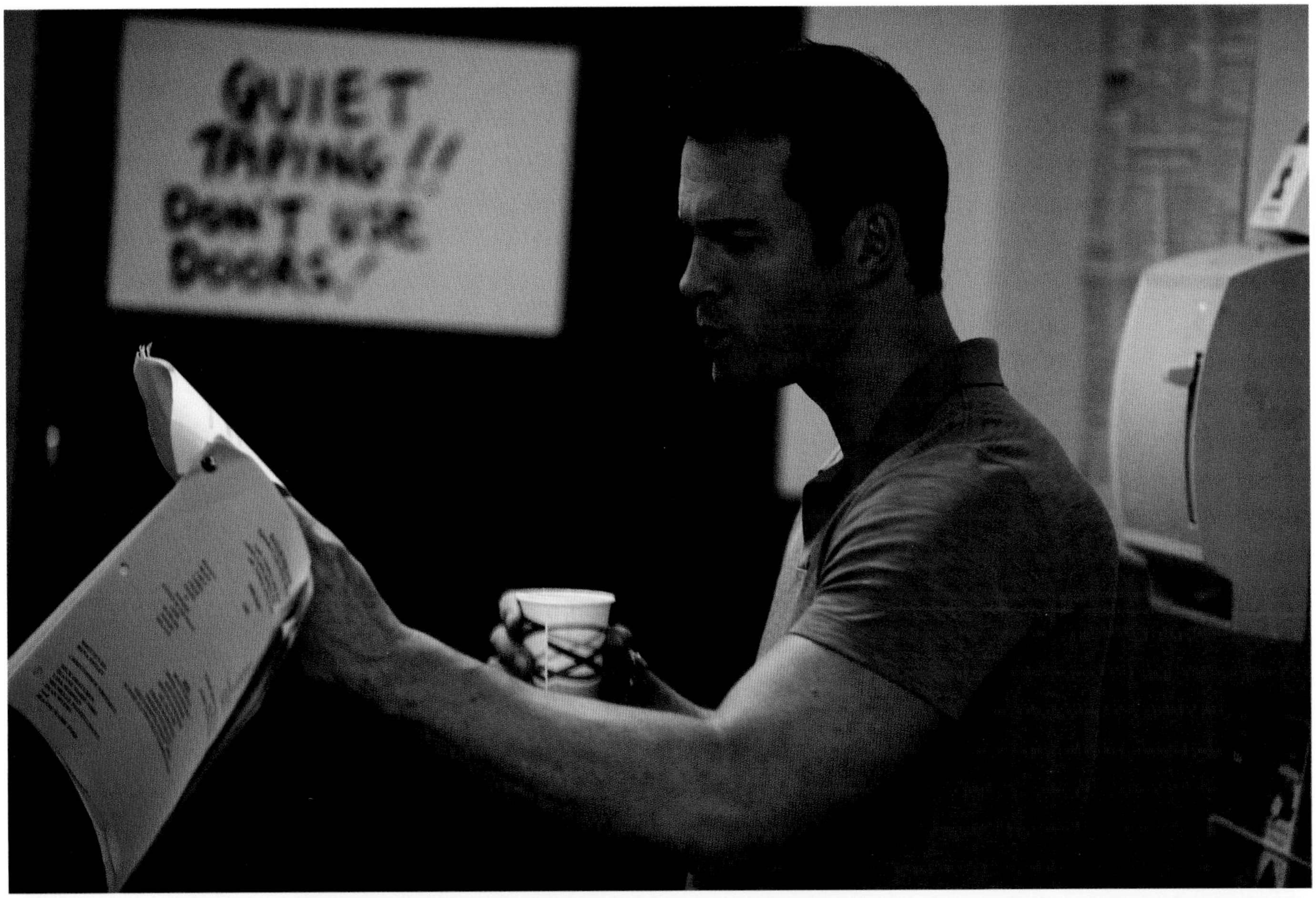
QUIET
TAPING!!
DON'T USE
DOORS!

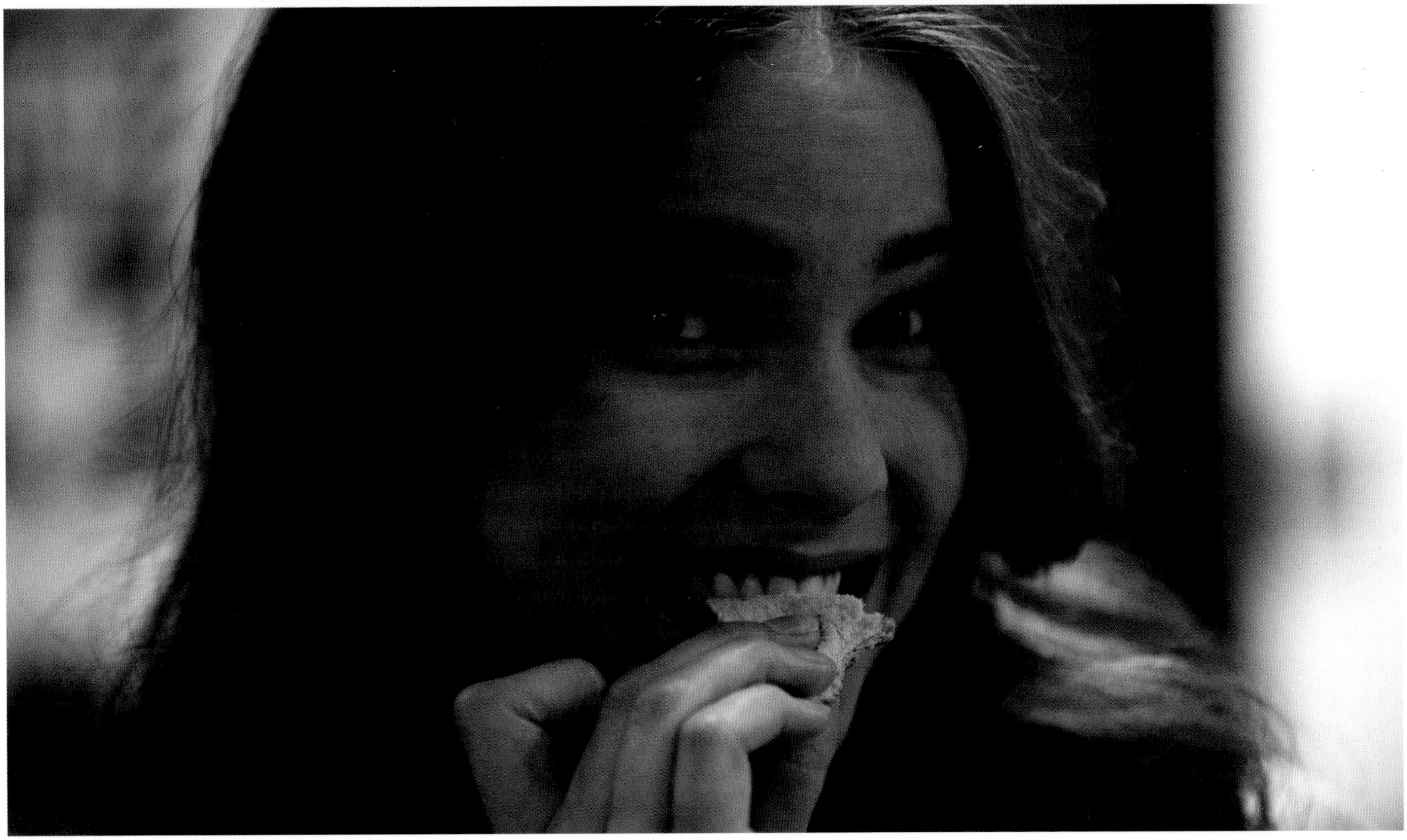

"BRADY"/ERIC MARTSOLF ON A LUNCH BREAK

LEFT:
"NATHAN"/MARK HAPKA
AND "STEPHANIE"/SHELLEY
HENNIG OUTSIDE
"MAGGIE'S" KITCHEN SET

RIGHT PAGE TOP:
"MARIE"/MAREE CHEATHAM
AND "STEPHANIE" OUTSIDE
"MAGGIE'S" KITCHEN SET

RIGHT PAGE BOTTOM:
"NATHAN AND STEPHANIE"
ON PIER SET

100

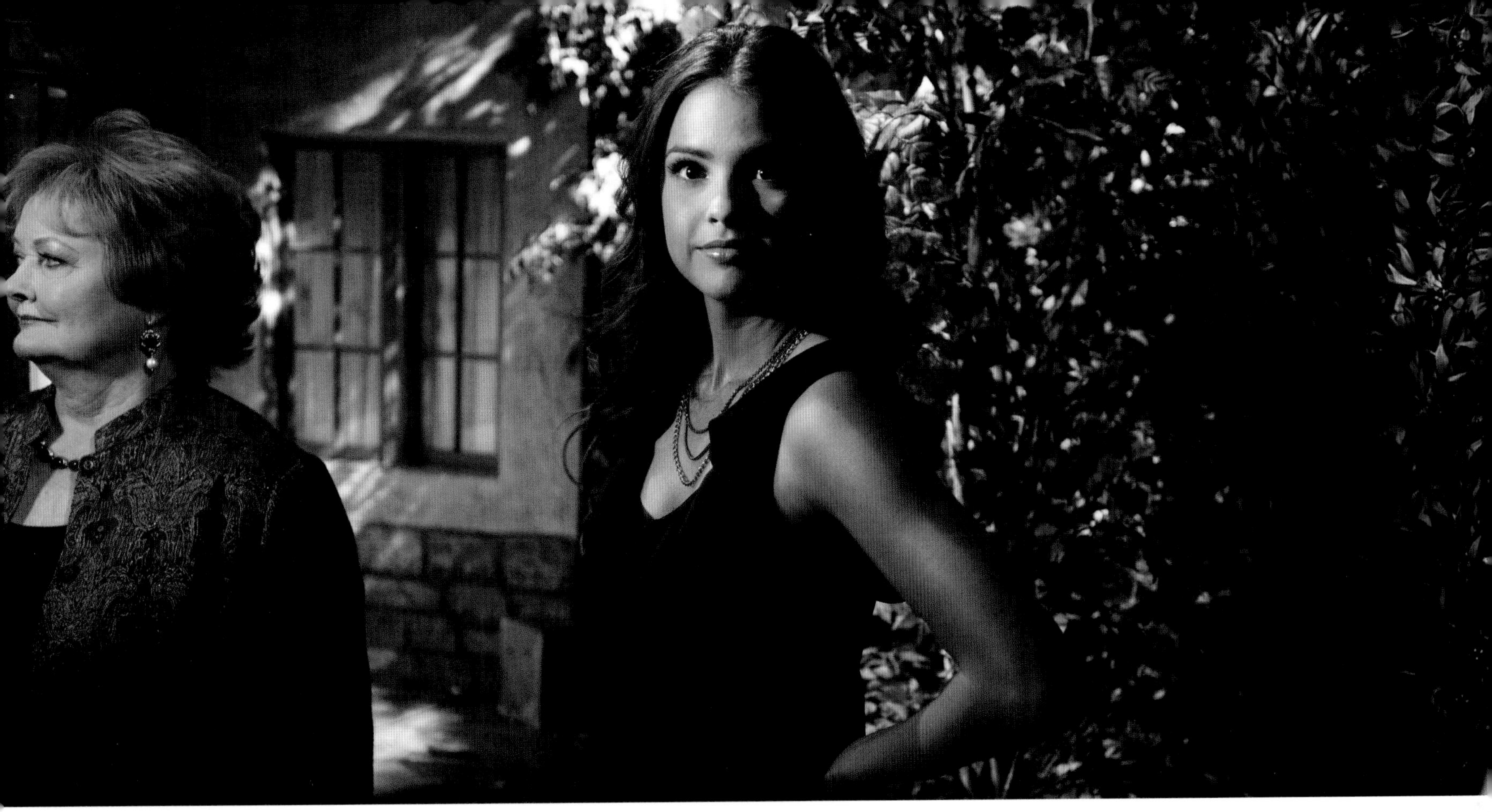

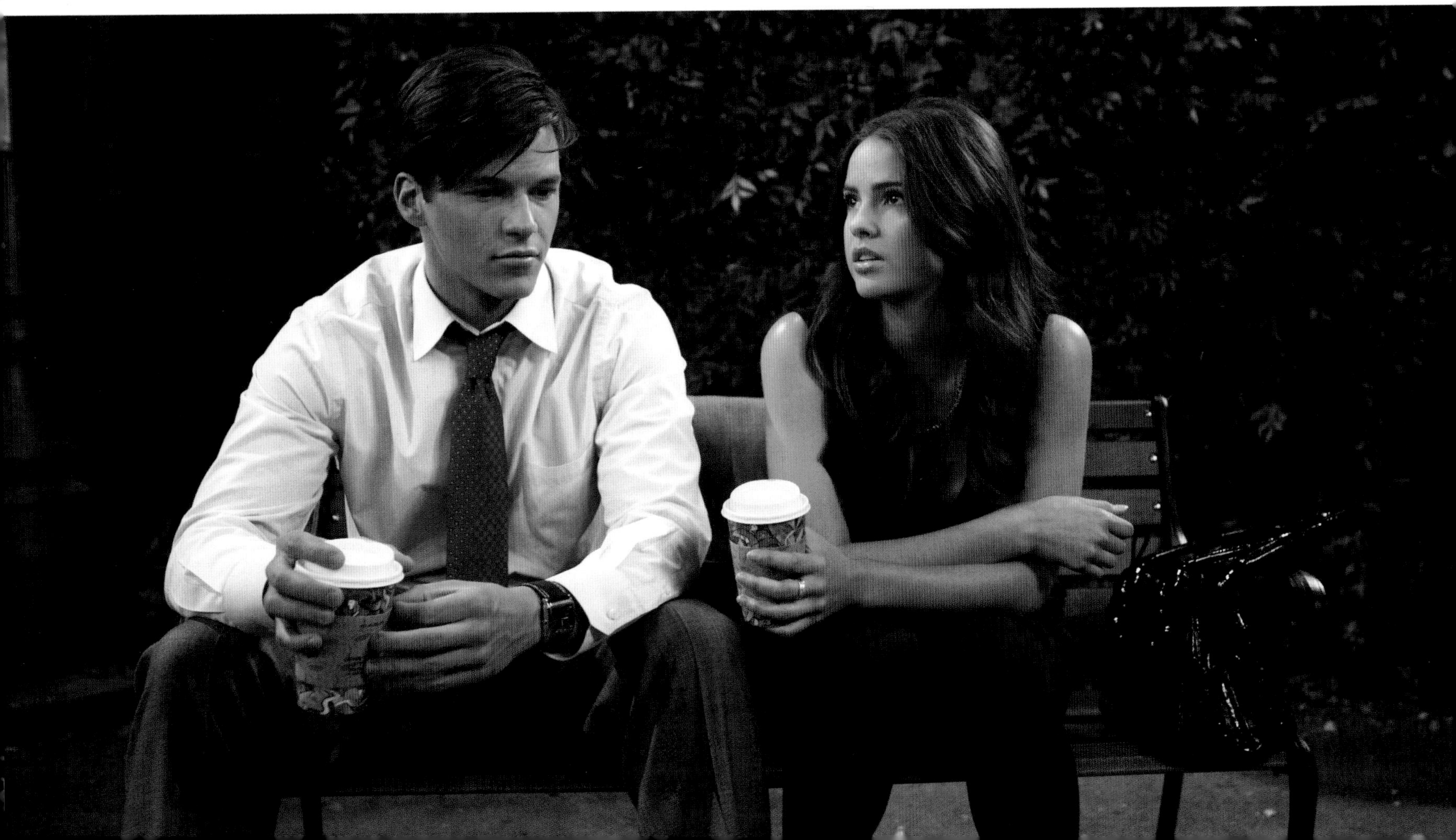

"CHLOE"/NADIA BJORLIN IN "DANIEL'S" APARTMENT

"BO"/PETER RECKELL CHECKING THE SCRIPT ONE MORE TIME BEFORE TAPING A SCENE

110 "CARLY"/CRYSTAL CHAPPELL, A QUIET MOMENT ON "BO/HOPE" LIVING ROOM SET

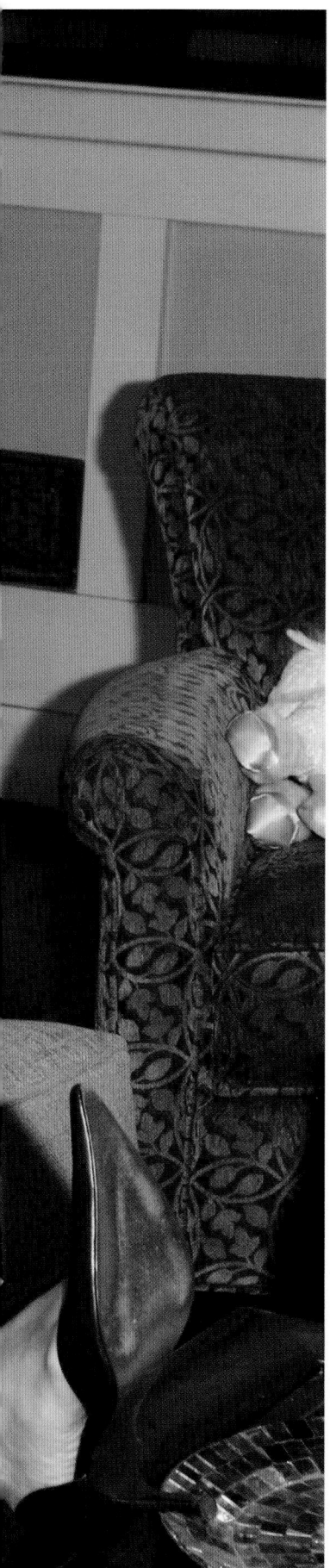

"CARLY" AND "VIVIAN"/LOUISE SOREL ON "SALEM HOSPITAL" SET

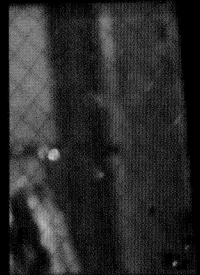

"WILL"/CHANDLER MASSEY FINISHED WITH HIS SCENES FOR THE DAY

As you can see by now, a lot of hard work goes into the making of *Days of our Lives*. The cast and crew are often scrambling from stage to stage and set to set. They are on the go constantly from their dressing rooms to hair and makeup and back to the set. With regular wardrobe changes, scene rehearsals, and last-minute read-throughs, the hallway between the stages is often the best place to capture the cast and crew in transition. There is never a dull moment, and rarely is there time to sit down and unwind. Enjoy as the tour continues...

STAGE MANAGER/GARY WENTE CALLING MOLLY BURNETT (RIGHT) TO STAGE

STAGE 2
IN
Stage
CLOSED SET
NO ADMITTANCE

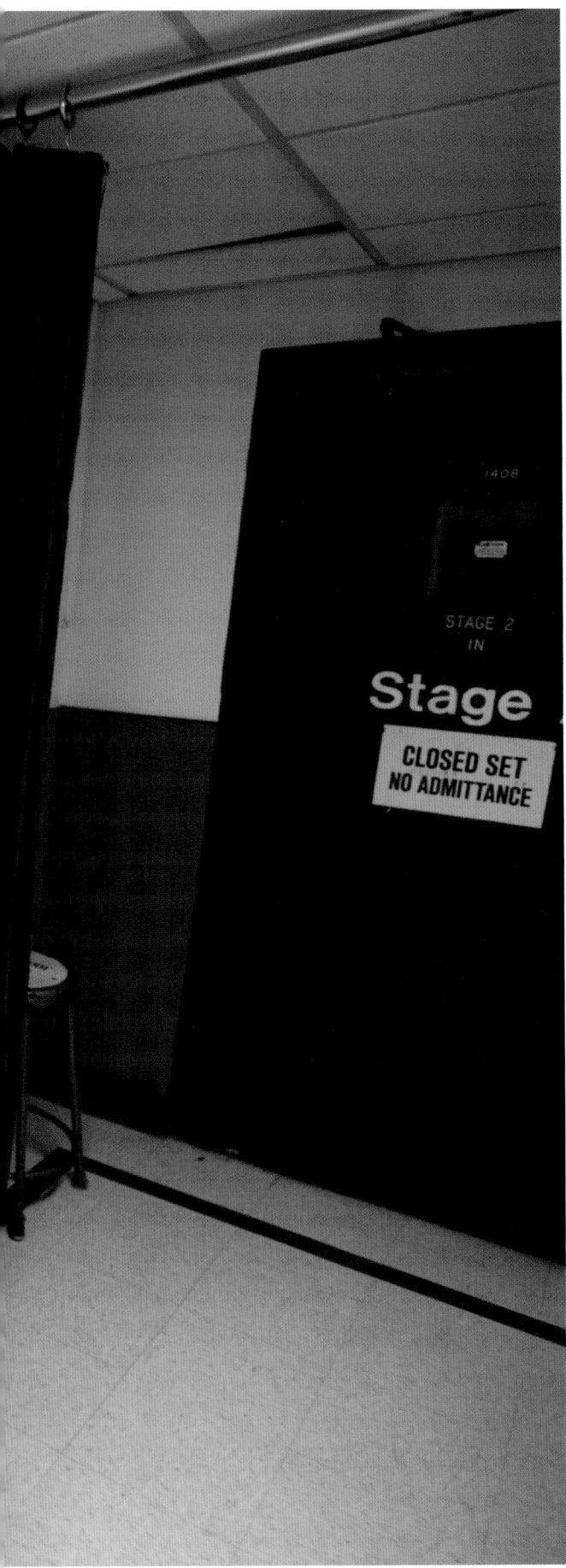

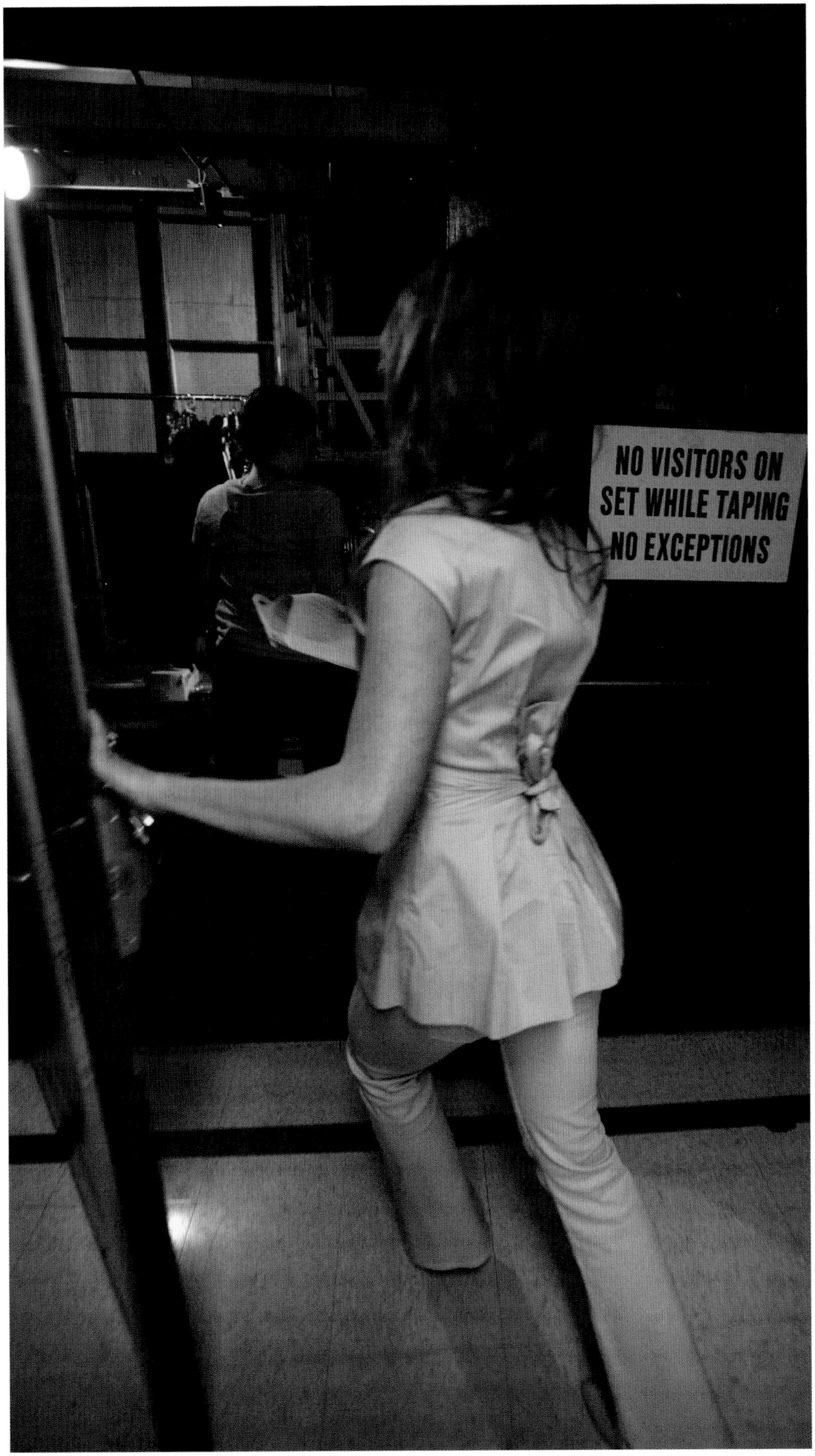
NO VISITORS ON
SET WHILE TAPING
NO EXCEPTIONS

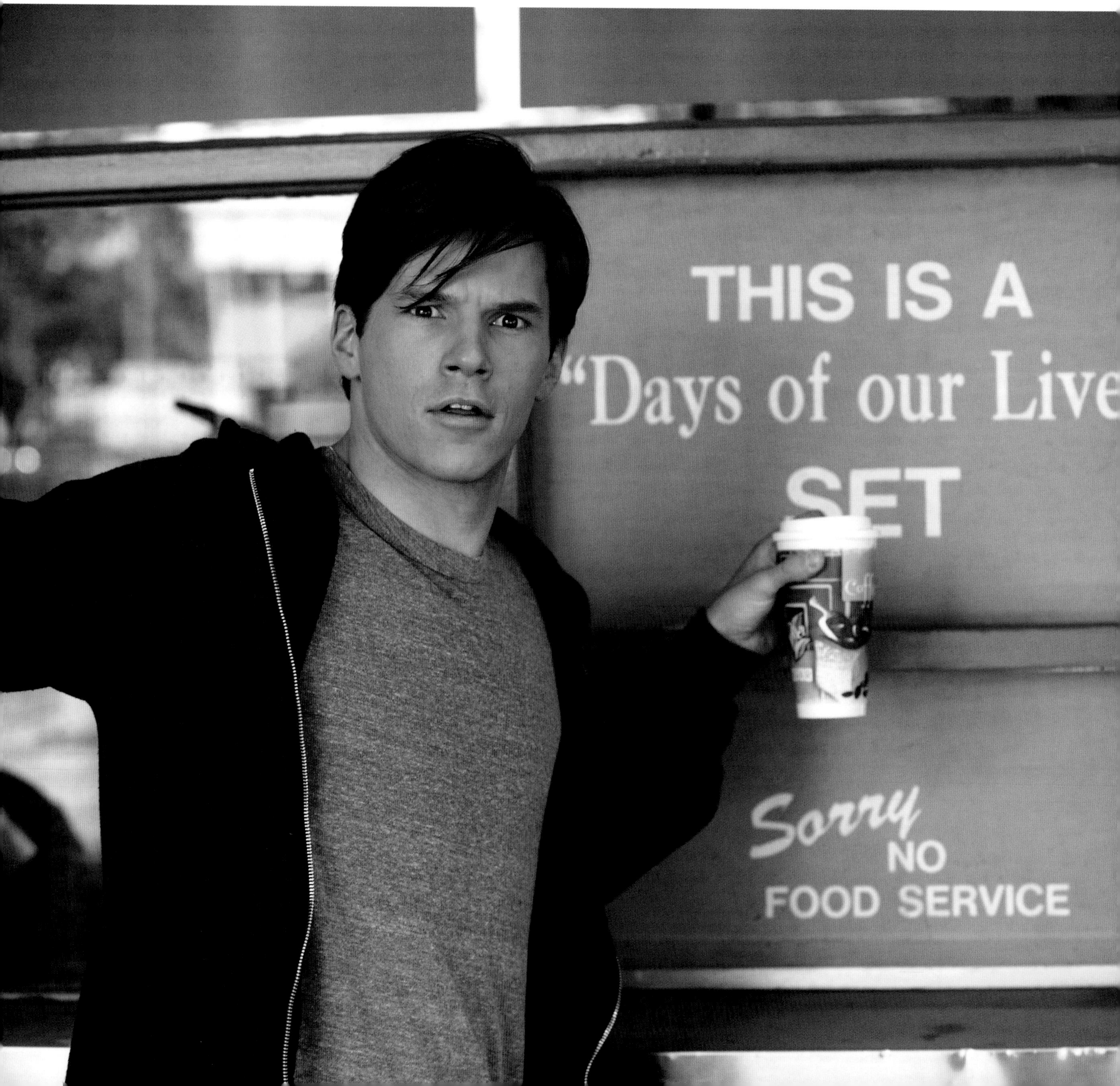
THIS IS A
"Days of our Live
SET
Sorry
NO
FOOD SERVICE

"NATHAN HORTON"/
MARK HAPKA ON "SALEM
PLACE" SET

121

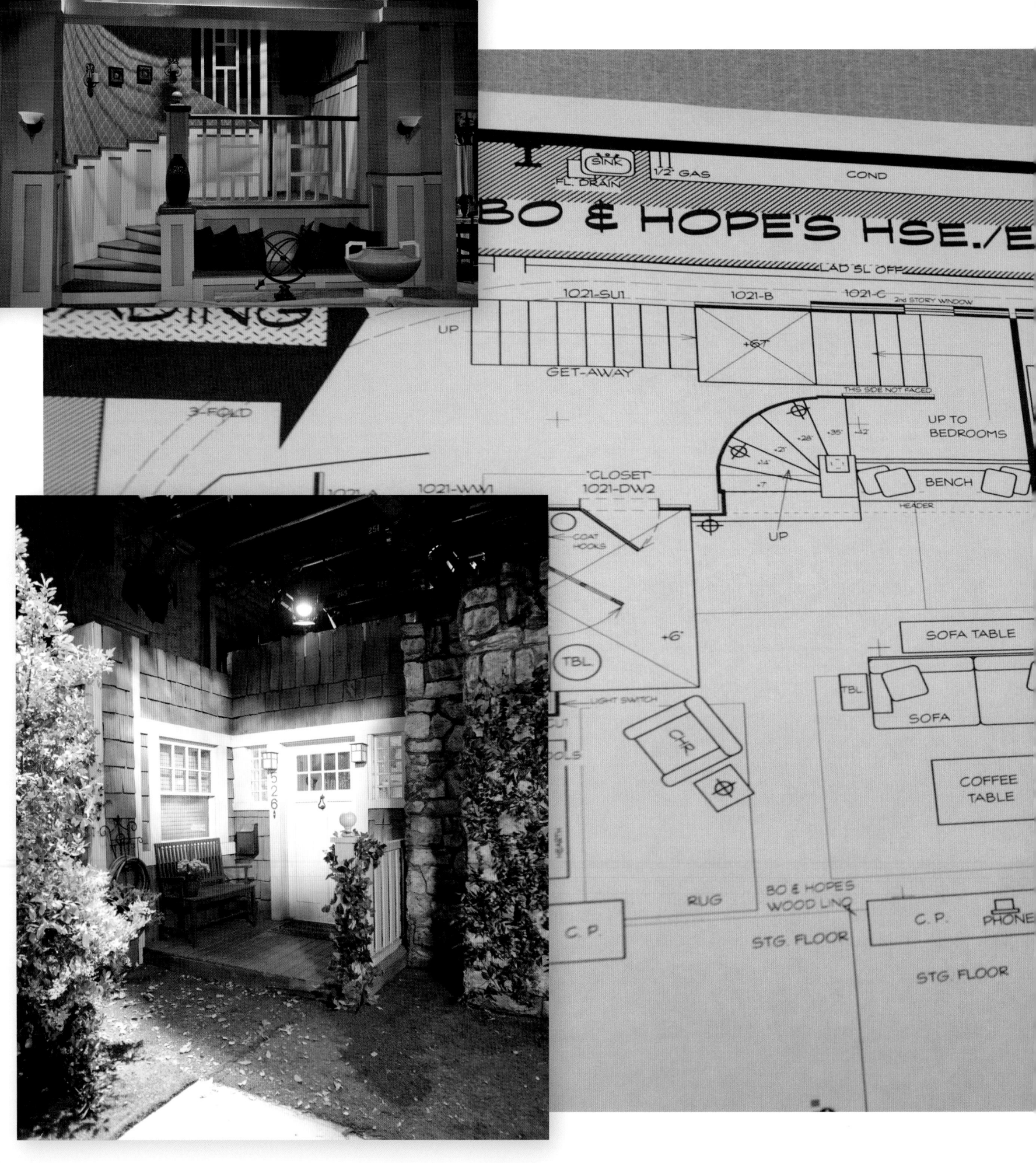

BO & HOPE'S HSE./E

SINK ½" GAS COND
FL. DRAIN

LAD 5L OFF

1021-SU1   1021-B   1021-C   2nd STORY WINDOW

UP

GET-AWAY

THIS SIDE NOT FACED

UP TO BEDROOMS

CLOSET
1021-DW2

BENCH

HEADER

COAT HOOKS

UP

SOFA TABLE

TBL

SOFA

CHR

COFFEE
TABLE

3-FOLD

1021-A   1021-WW1

TBL

LIGHT SWITCH

C.P.

RUG

BO & HOPES
WOOD LNG

STG FLOOR

C.P.   PHONE

STG FLOOR

530

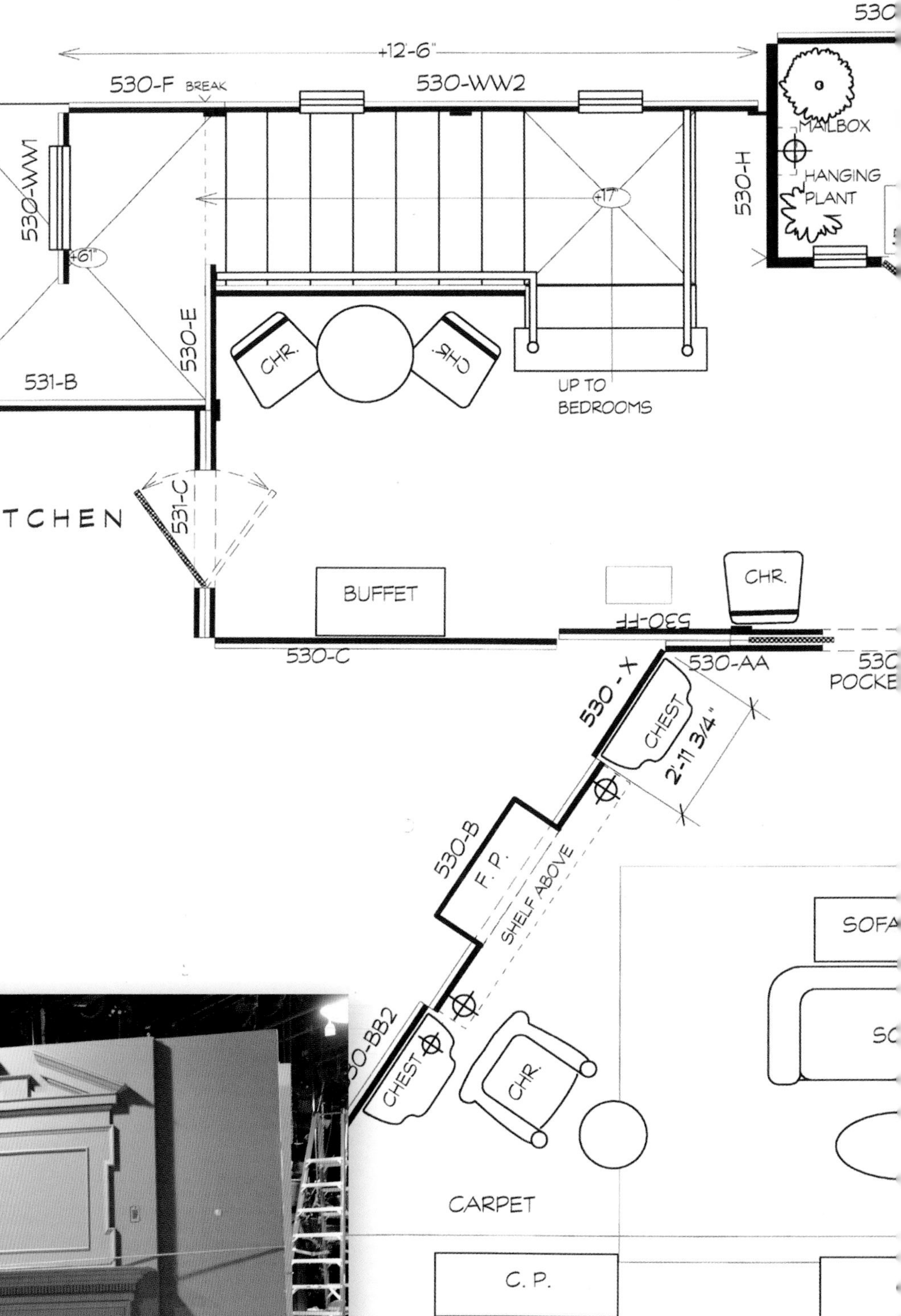

+12-6"

530-F BREAK

530-WW2

530-WW1

530

MAILBOX

HANGING PLANT

530-H

+61"

+17

530-E

531-B

CHR.

CHR.

UP TO BEDROOMS

KITCHEN

531-C

BUFFET

CHR.

530-FF

530-C

530-X

530-AA

530 POCKE

CHEST

2'-11 3/4"

530-B

F.P.

SHELF ABOVE

SOFA

SO

530-BB2

CHEST

CHR.

CARPET

C.P.

VING ROOM

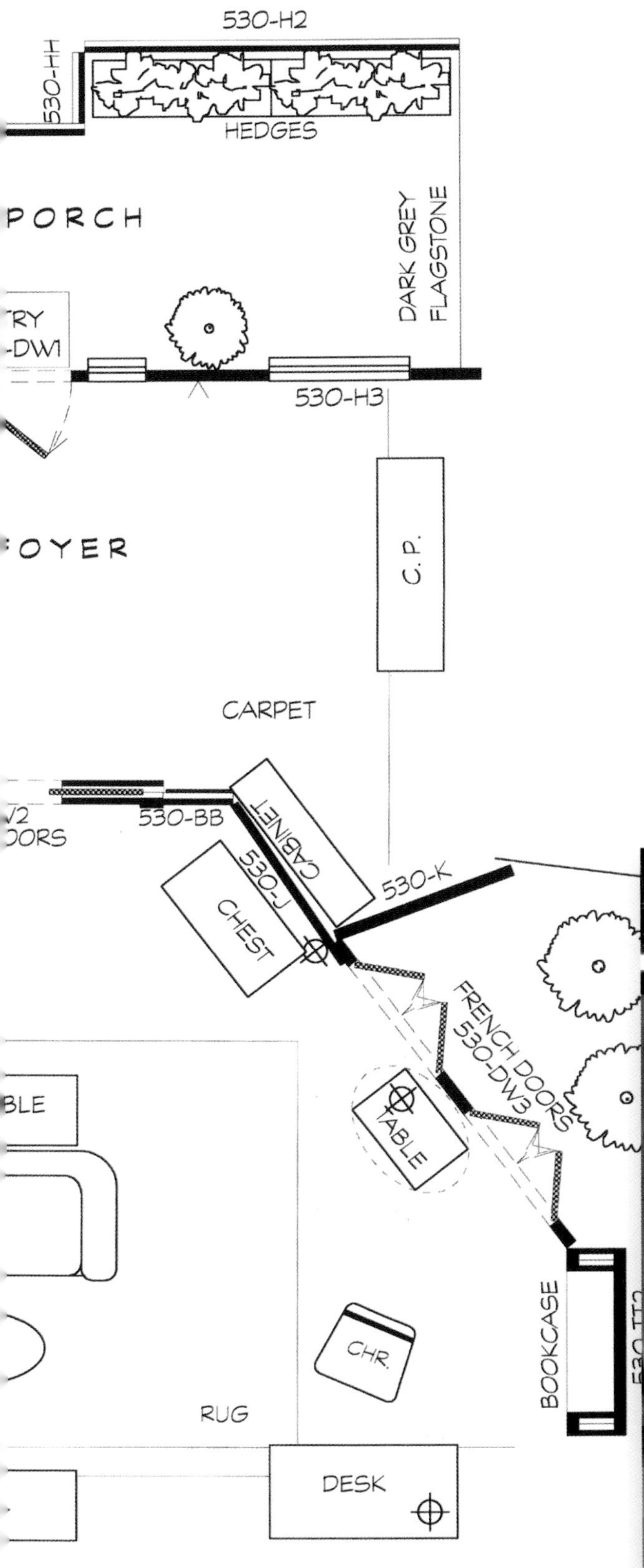

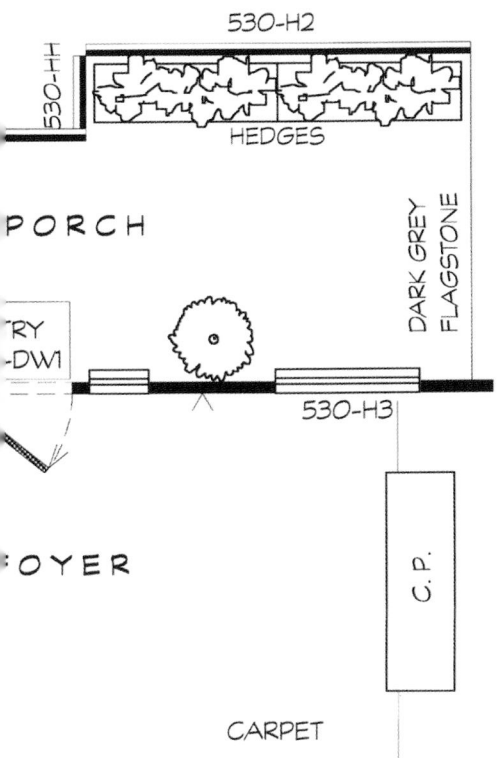

530-HH

530-H2

HEDGES

PORCH

DARK GREY FLAGSTONE

RY-DW1

530-H3

FOYER

C.P.

CARPET

V2
OORS

530-BB

CHEST

530-J CABINET

530-K

FRENCH DOORS 530-DW3

TABLE

BLE

BOOKCASE

530-TT2

CHR.

RUG

DESK

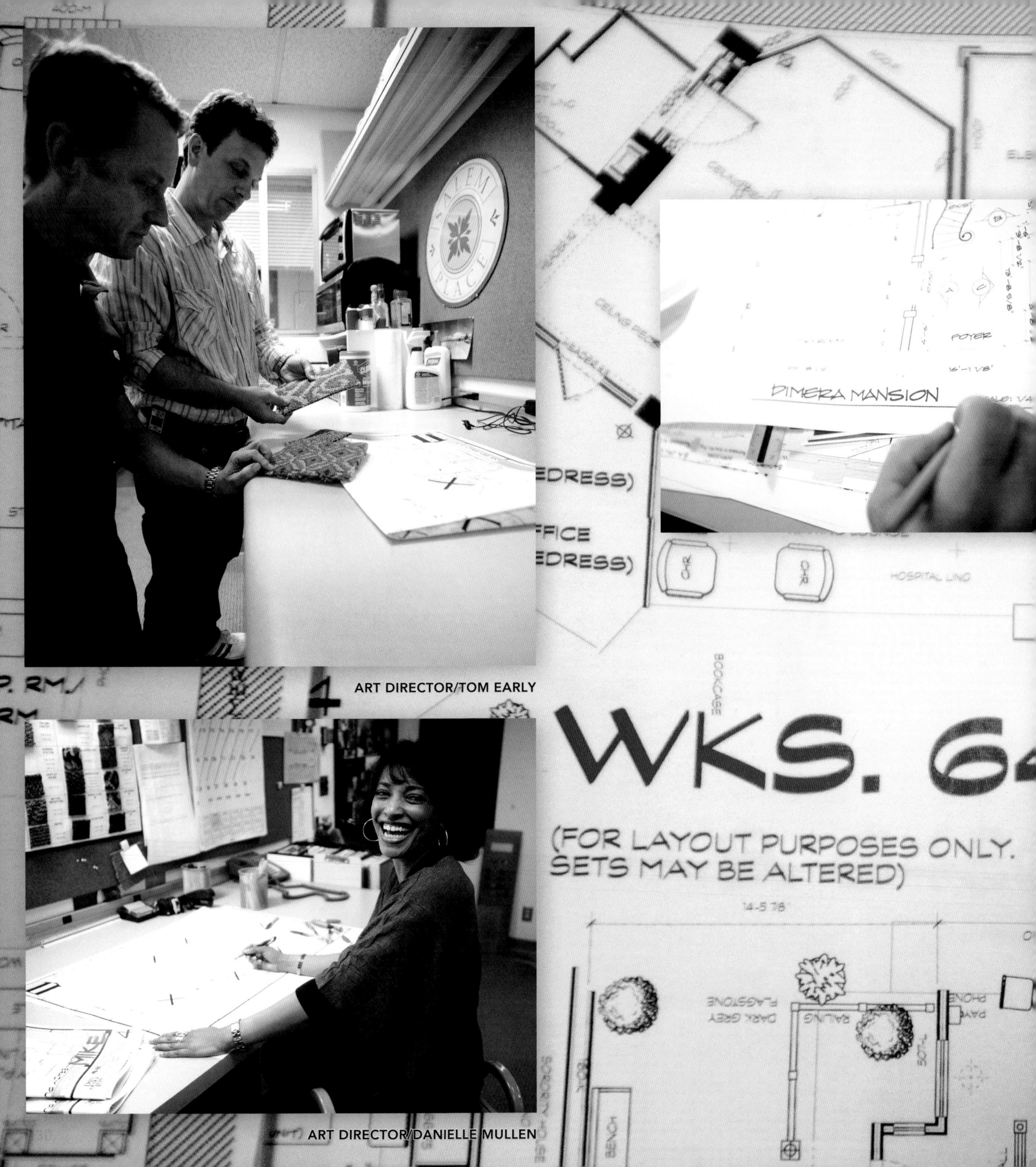

ART DIRECTOR/TOM EARLY

ART DIRECTOR/DANIELLE MULLEN

DIMERA MANSION

WKS. 6

(FOR LAYOUT PURPOSES ONLY.
SETS MAY BE ALTERED)

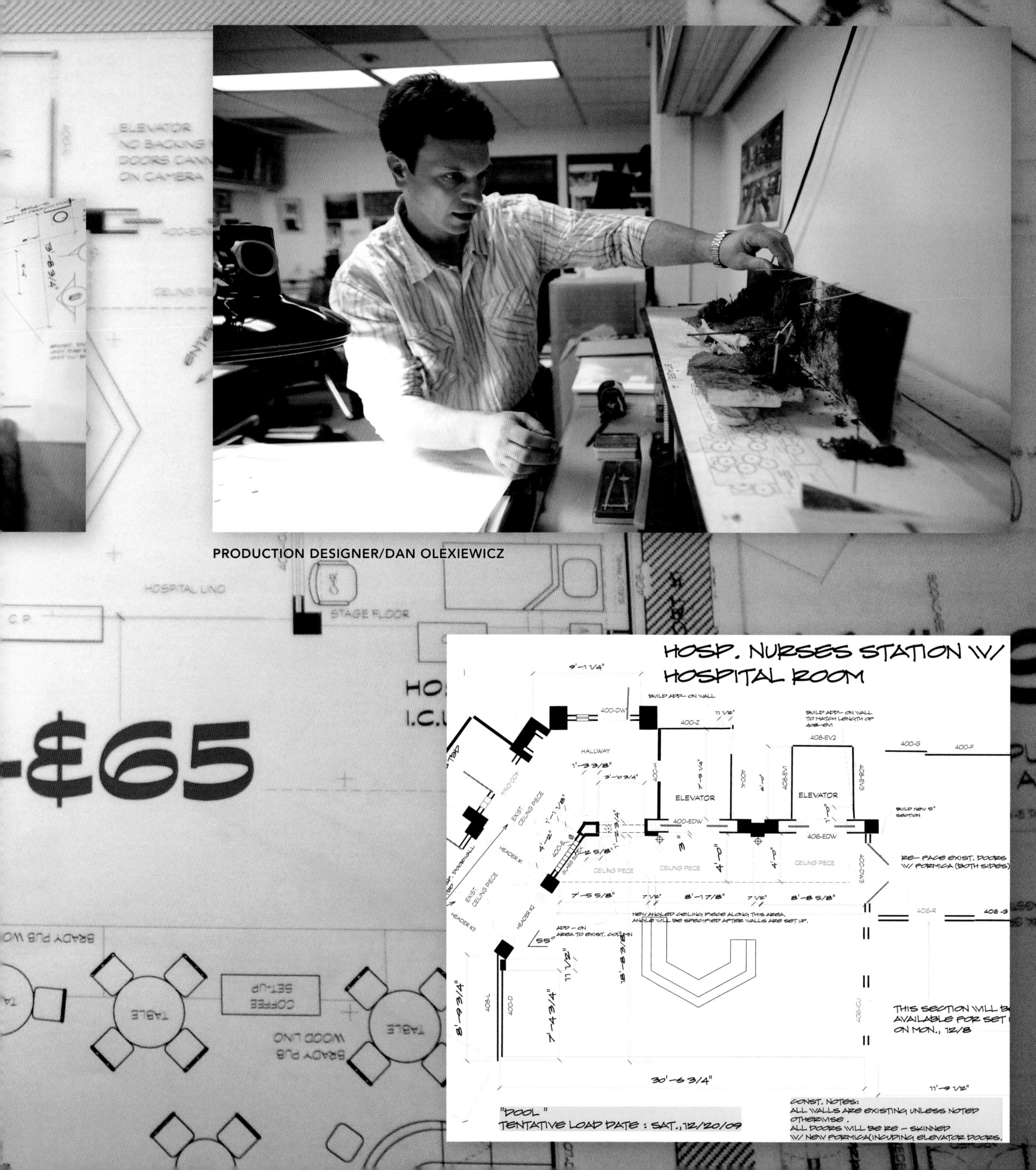

PRODUCTION DESIGNER/DAN OLEXIEWICZ

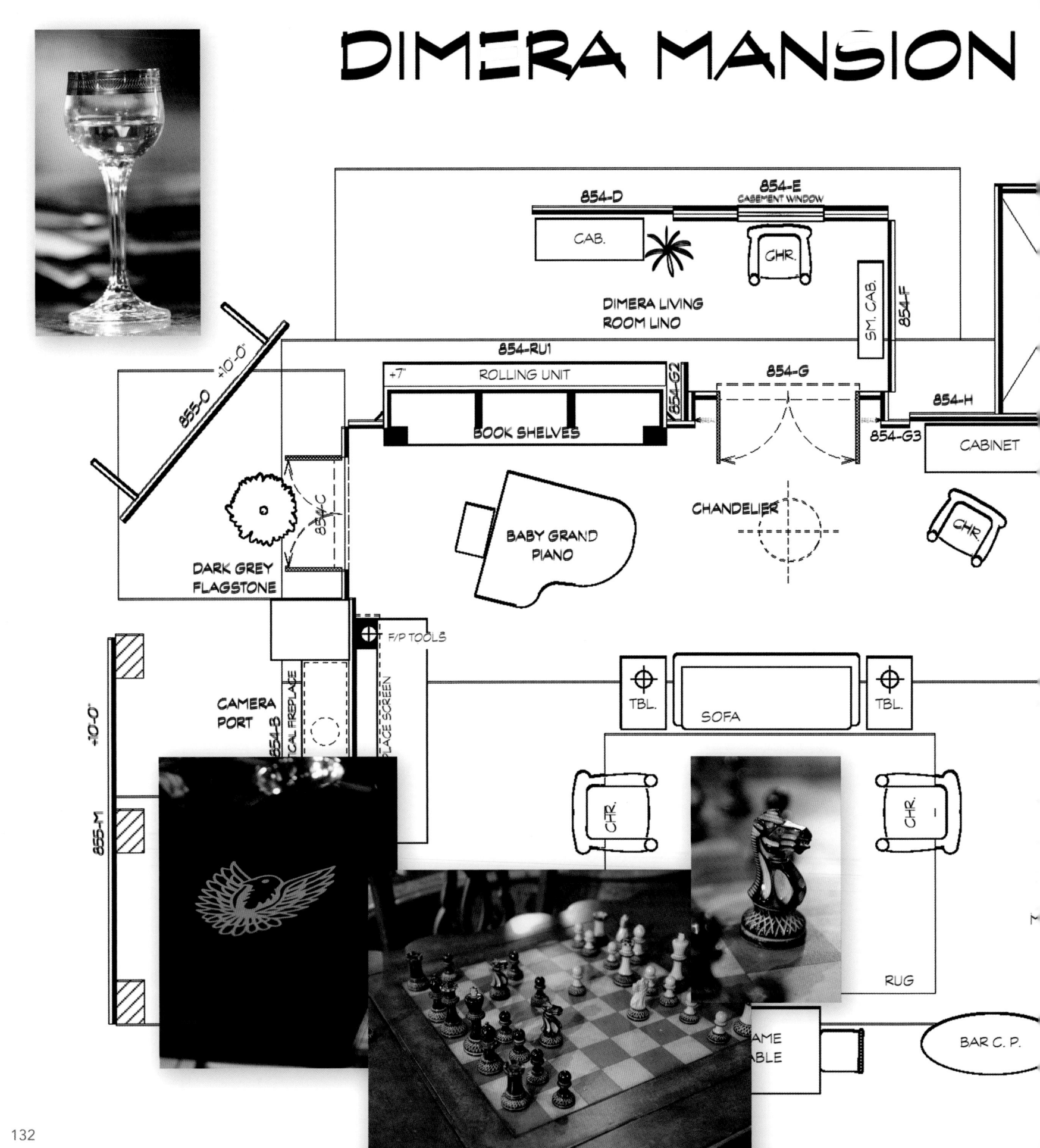

DIMERA MANSION

854-D

854-E
CASEMENT WINDOW

CAB.

CHR.

SM. CAB.

854-F

DIMERA LIVING
ROOM LINO

854-RU1

+7"   ROLLING UNIT

854-G2

854-G

854-H

BOOK SHELVES

854-G3

CABINET

855-0   +10'-0"

854-C

CHANDELIER

CHR.

DARK GREY
FLAGSTONE

BABY GRAND
PIANO

F/P TOOLS

TBL.

SOFA

TBL.

+10'-0"

CAMERA
PORT

854-B

CAL FIREPLACE

LACE SCREEN

855-M

CHR.

CHR.

RUG

AME
ABLE

BAR C. P.

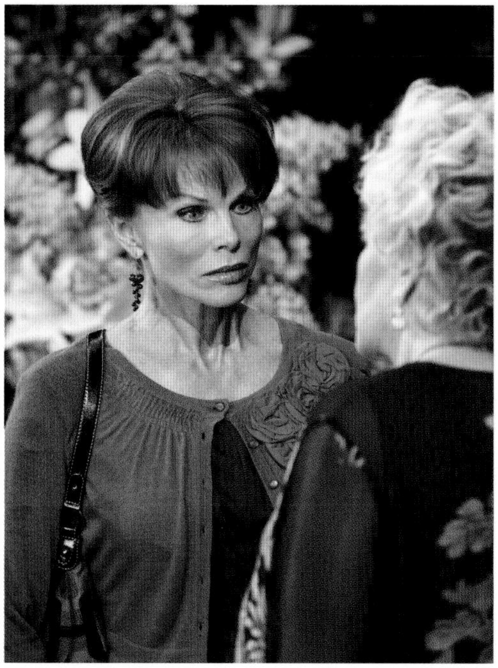
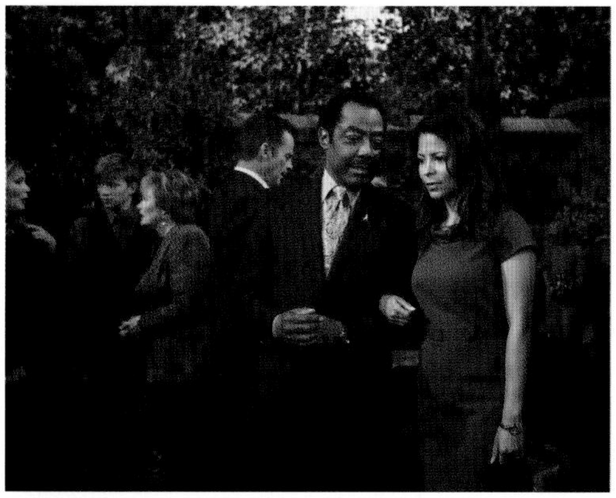
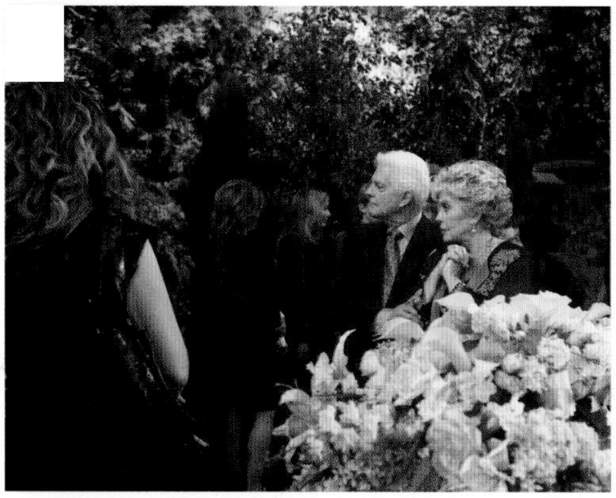
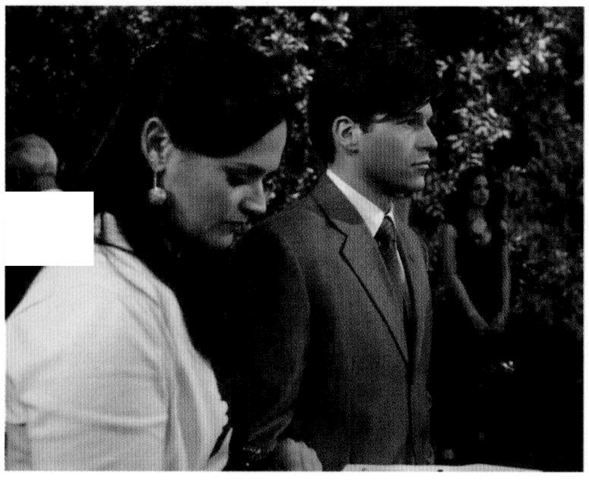
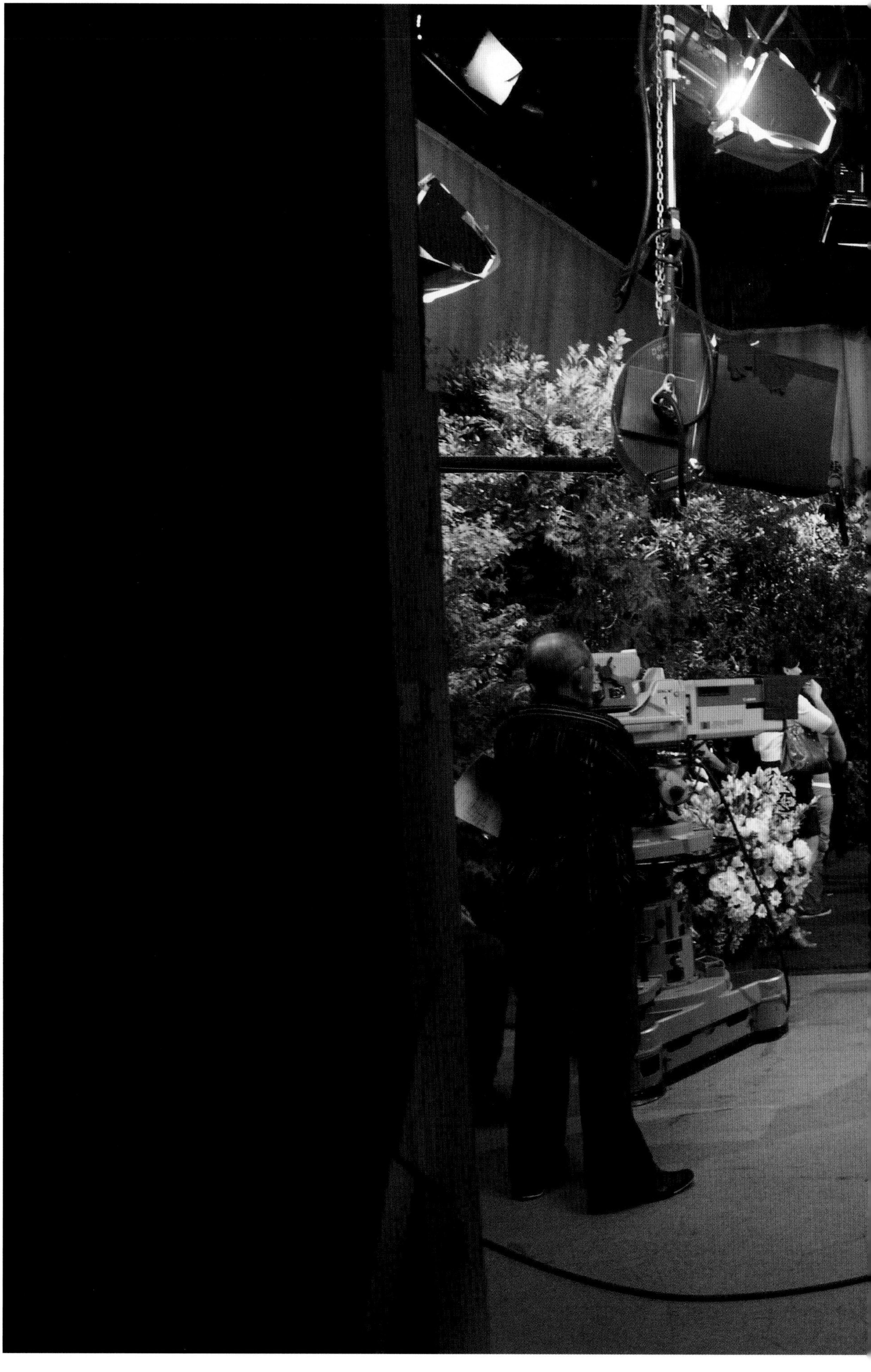

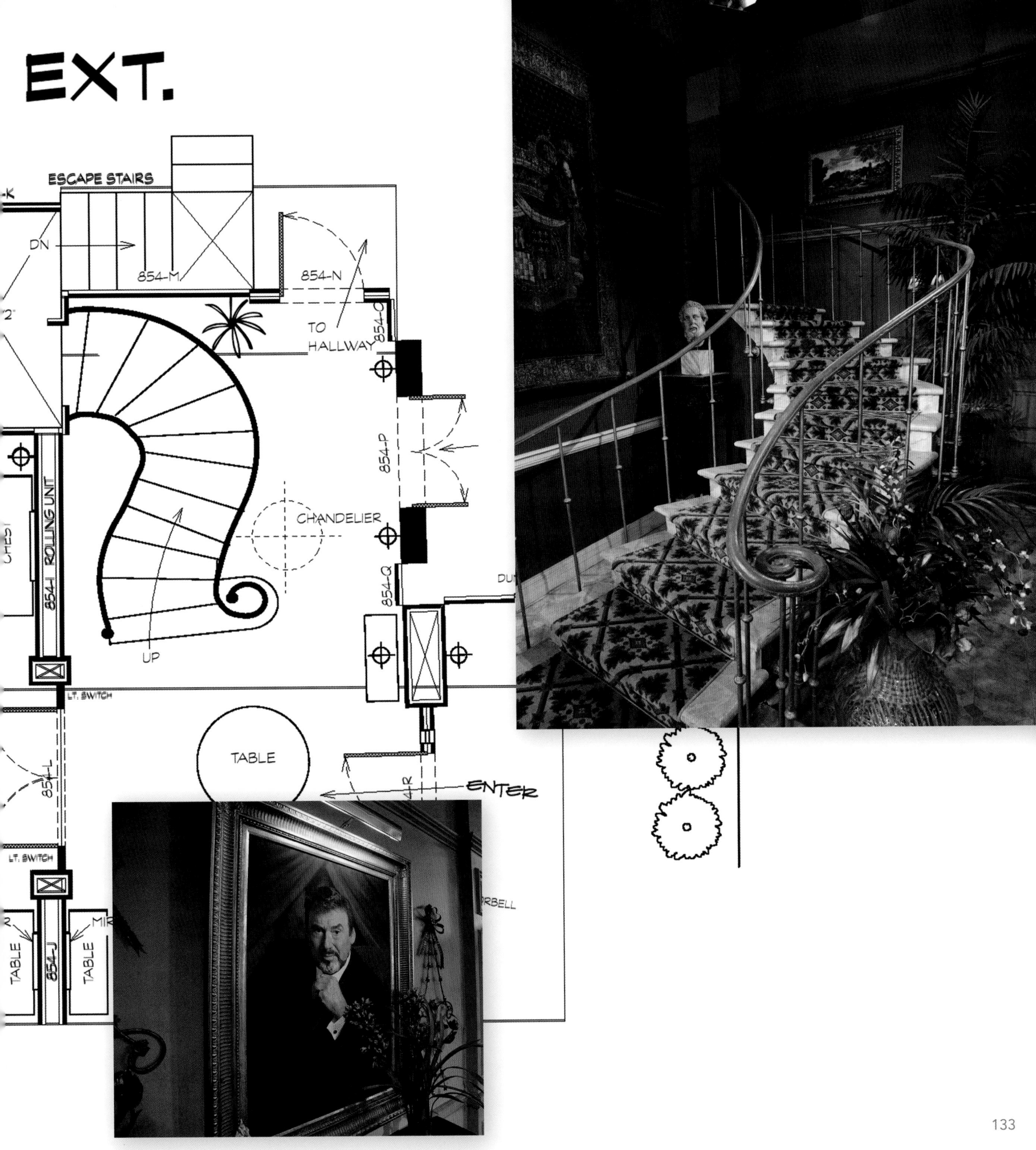

EXT.

ESCAPE STAIRS

K

DN

854-M

854-N

2'

TO
HALLWAY

854-O

CHEST

854-I ROLLING UNIT

854-P

CHANDELIER

854-Q

UP

DU

LT. SWITCH

TABLE

R

ENTER

854-L

LT. SWITCH

854-J

TABLE   MIR

TABLE   TABLE

ORBELL

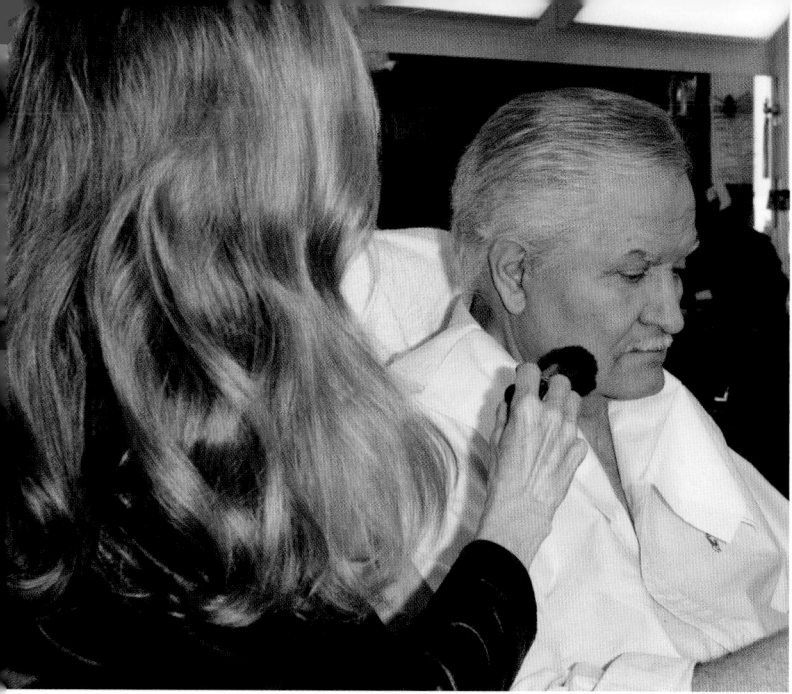

HEAD MAKEUP/GAIL HOPKINS GIVES "VICTOR"/
JOHN ANISTON A QUICK TOUCH-UP BEFORE
GOING ON THE "KIRIAKIS" SET

"CHAD"/CASEY JON DEIDRICK WAITING FOR HAIR AND MAKEUP

"ROMAN"/JOSH TAYLOR PREPARING FOR HIS NEXT SCENE

"RAFE"/GALEN GERING IN HIS DRESSING ROOM

"CAROLINE"/PEGGY MCCAY ON THE "BRADY PUB" SET   143

EXECUTIVE PRODUCER/KEN CORDAY TALKS TO "JULIE"/SUSAN SEAFORTH HAYES AND "SAMI"/ALISON SWEENEY BETWEEN STAGES 2 AND 4 AS SUSAN AND ALISON WAIT TO BE CALLED ON SET

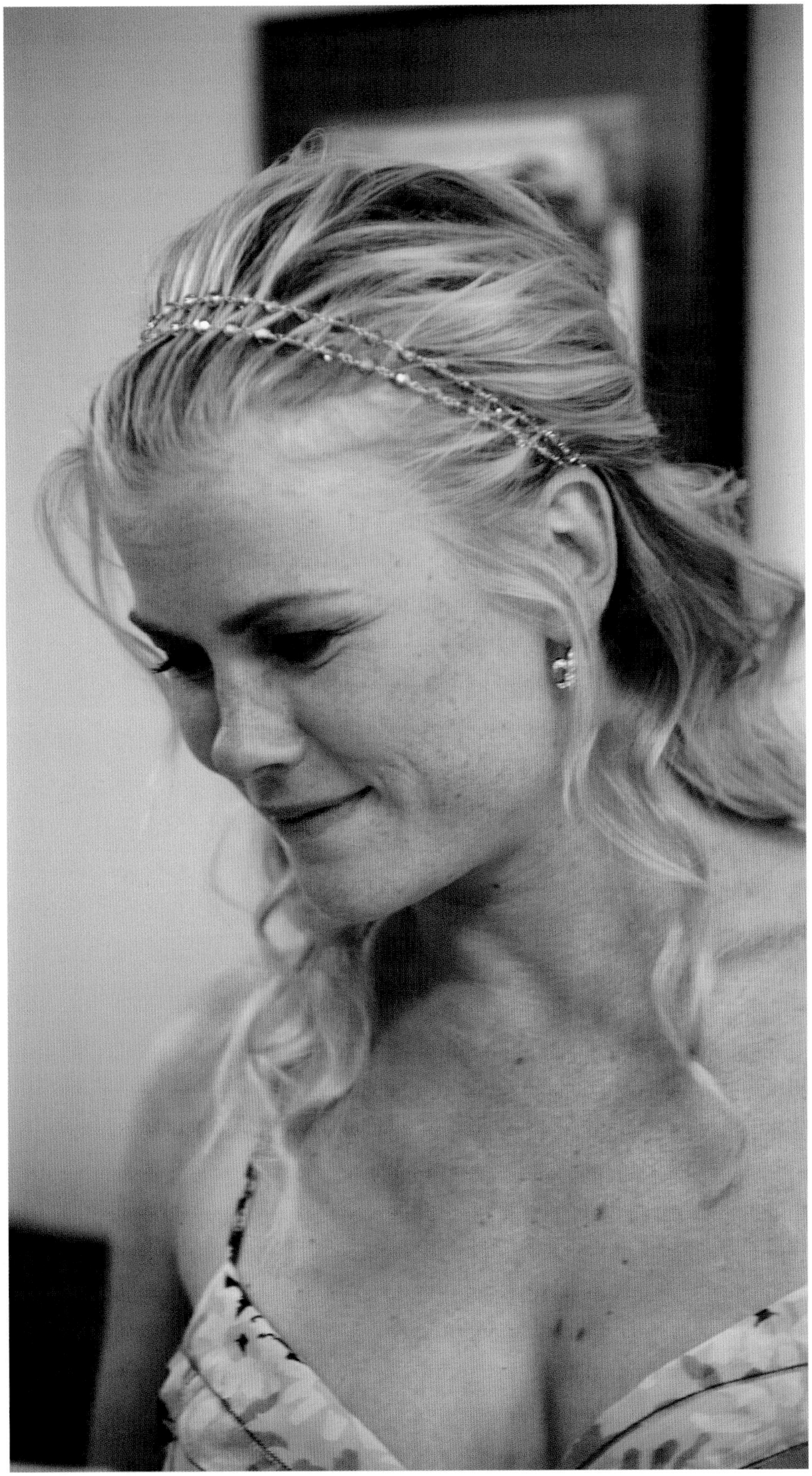

"VIVIAN"/LOUISE SOREL AND HAIR STYLIST/MARGARET PUGA

"DOUG"/BILL HAYES AND "ABE"/JAMES
REYNOLDS ON THE "HORTON" KITCHEN SET

...BACK ON STAGE READY
TO TAPE A SCENE

"DANIEL"/SHAWN CHRISTIAN
IN THE MIDDLE OF A QUICK
WARDROBE CHANGE

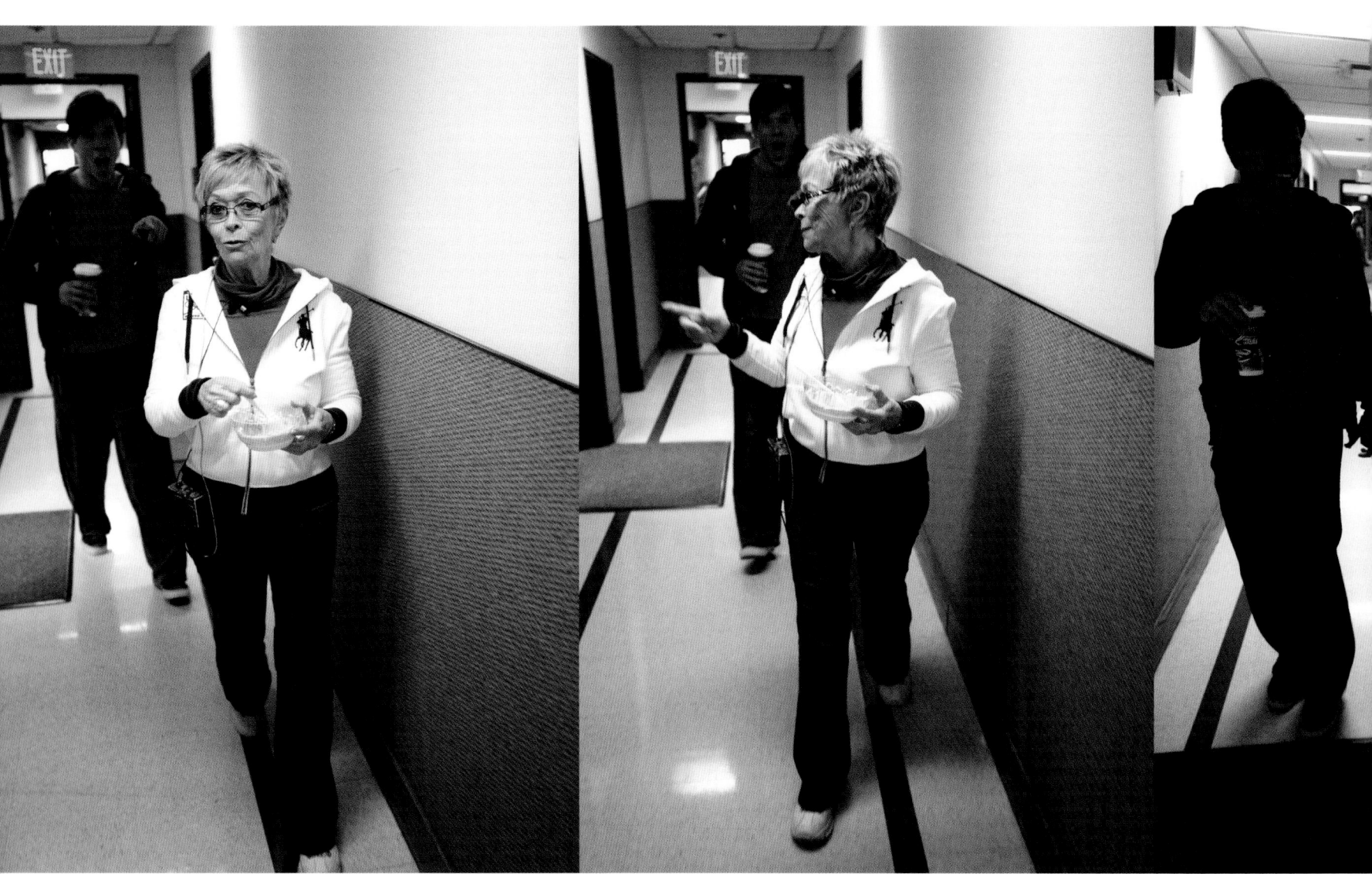

"NATHAN HORTON"/MARK HAPKA SNEAKING UP ON STAGE MANAGER/FRANCESCA BELLINI DE SIMONE

"PHILIP"/JAY JOHNSON READING LINES IN HAIR AND MAKEUP

SHAWN CRASHES MOLLY AND
ARIANNE'S NAP BETWEEN SCENES
IN ARIANNE'S DRESSING ROOM

"ADRIENNE"/JUDI EVANS ON THE AIRPLANE
SET USED BY "RAFE" AND "SHANE" TO FLY
BACK TO SALEM FOR "ALICE'S" MEMORIAL

"NICOLE"/ARIANNE ZUCKER

"DOUG"/BILL HAYES

"KAYLA"/MARY BETH EVANS AND
"STEPHANIE"/SHELLEY HENNIG WAITING
TO BE CALLED TO SET

"NICOLE"/ARIANNE ZUCKER IN HER DRESSING ROOM

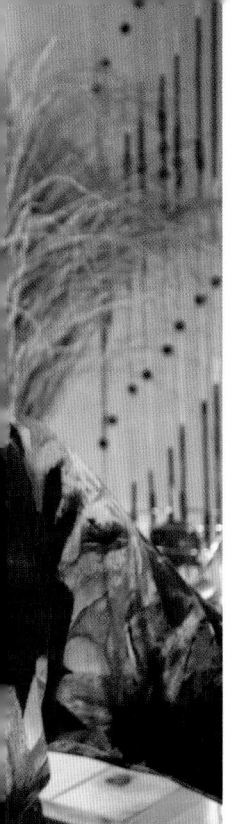

195

DAYS OF OUR LIVES
D.O.O.L HORTON
LIVING ROOM

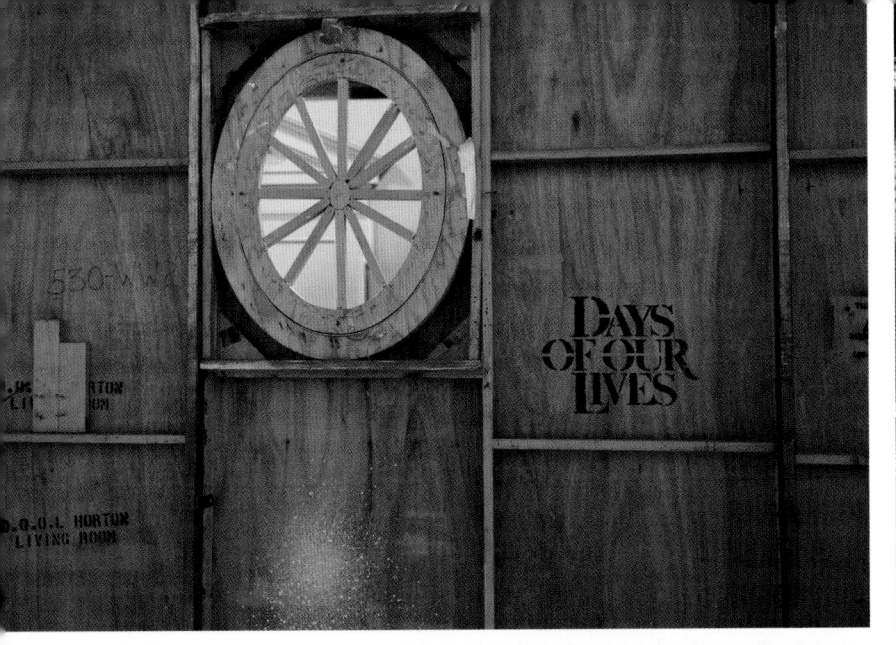

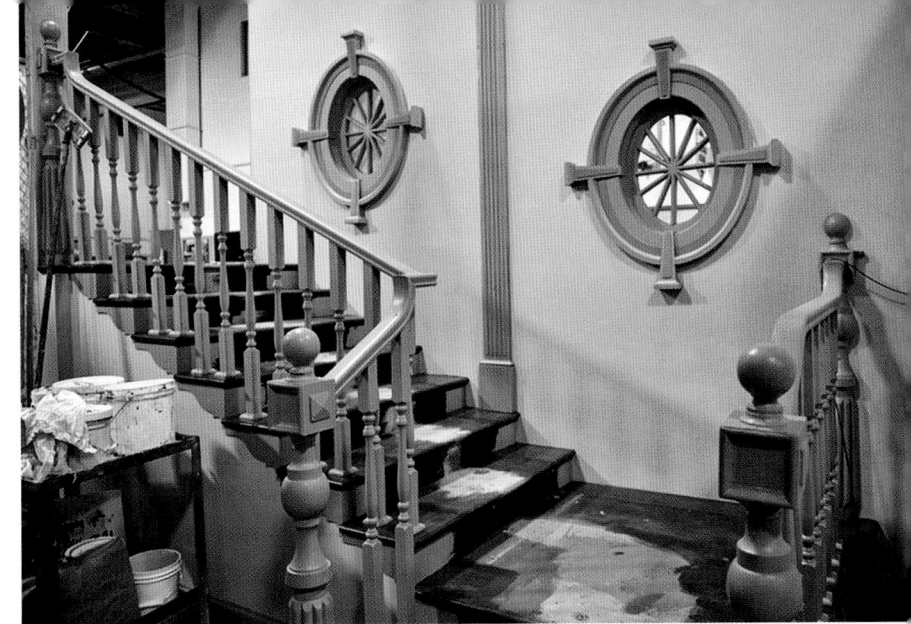

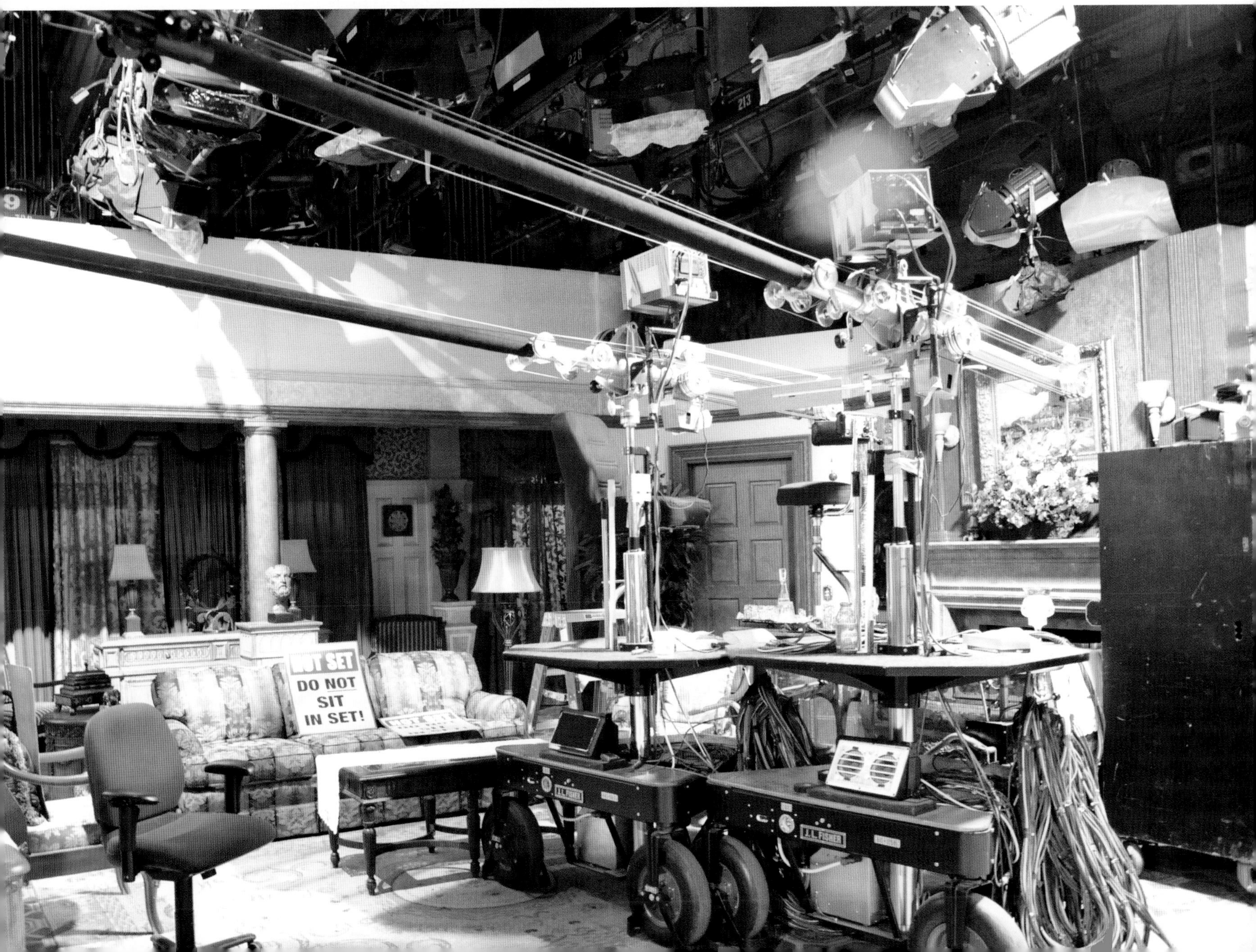
HOT SET
DO NOT
SIT
IN SET!
J.L. FISHER

"BO AND HOPE"/PETER
RECKELL AND KRISTIAN
ALFONSO ON THEIR SET
AS LIGHTING DIRECTOR
MAKES A MINOR CHANGE

"CARRIE"/CHRISTIE CLARK BACK FOR "ALICE'S" MEMORIAL

CORDAY
PRODUCTIONS, INC.

DAYS OF OUR LIVE

OOPS! CAUGHT PICKING OUT ONE MORE PIECE OF JEWELRY

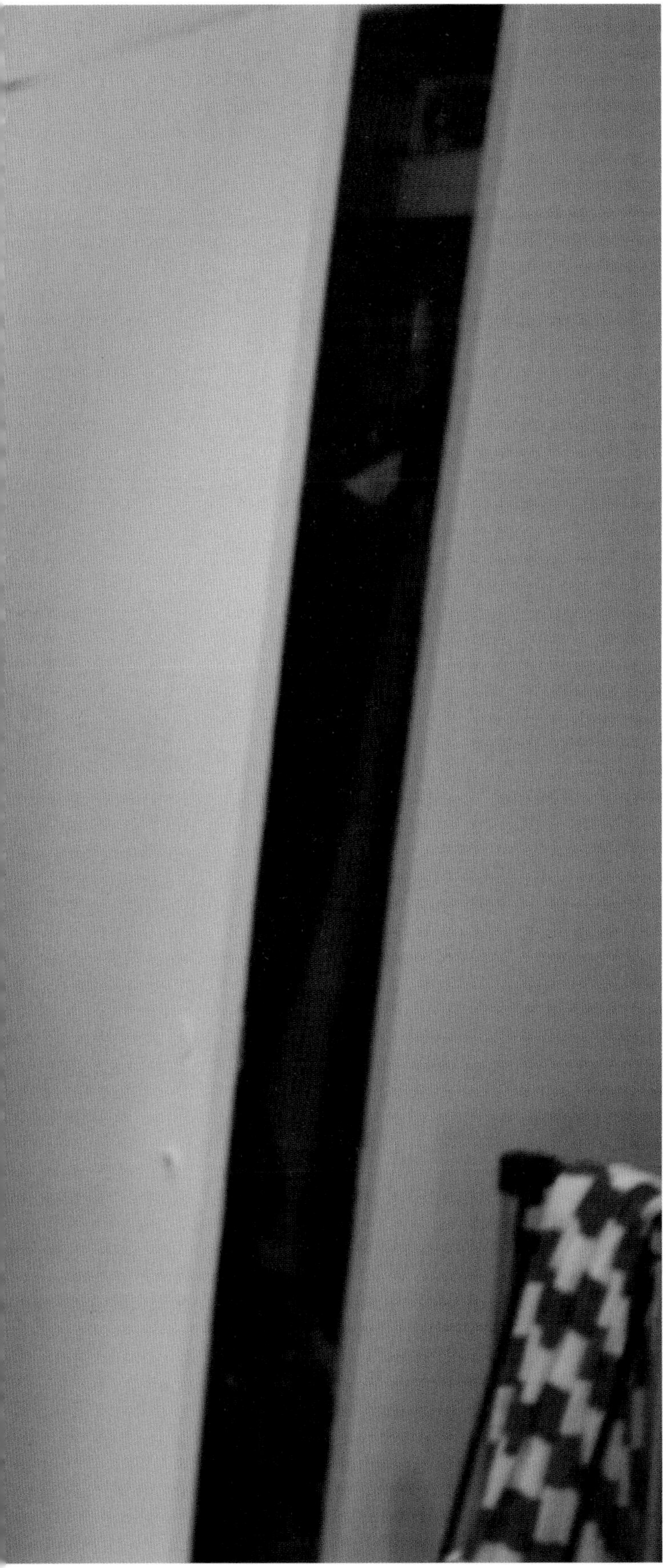

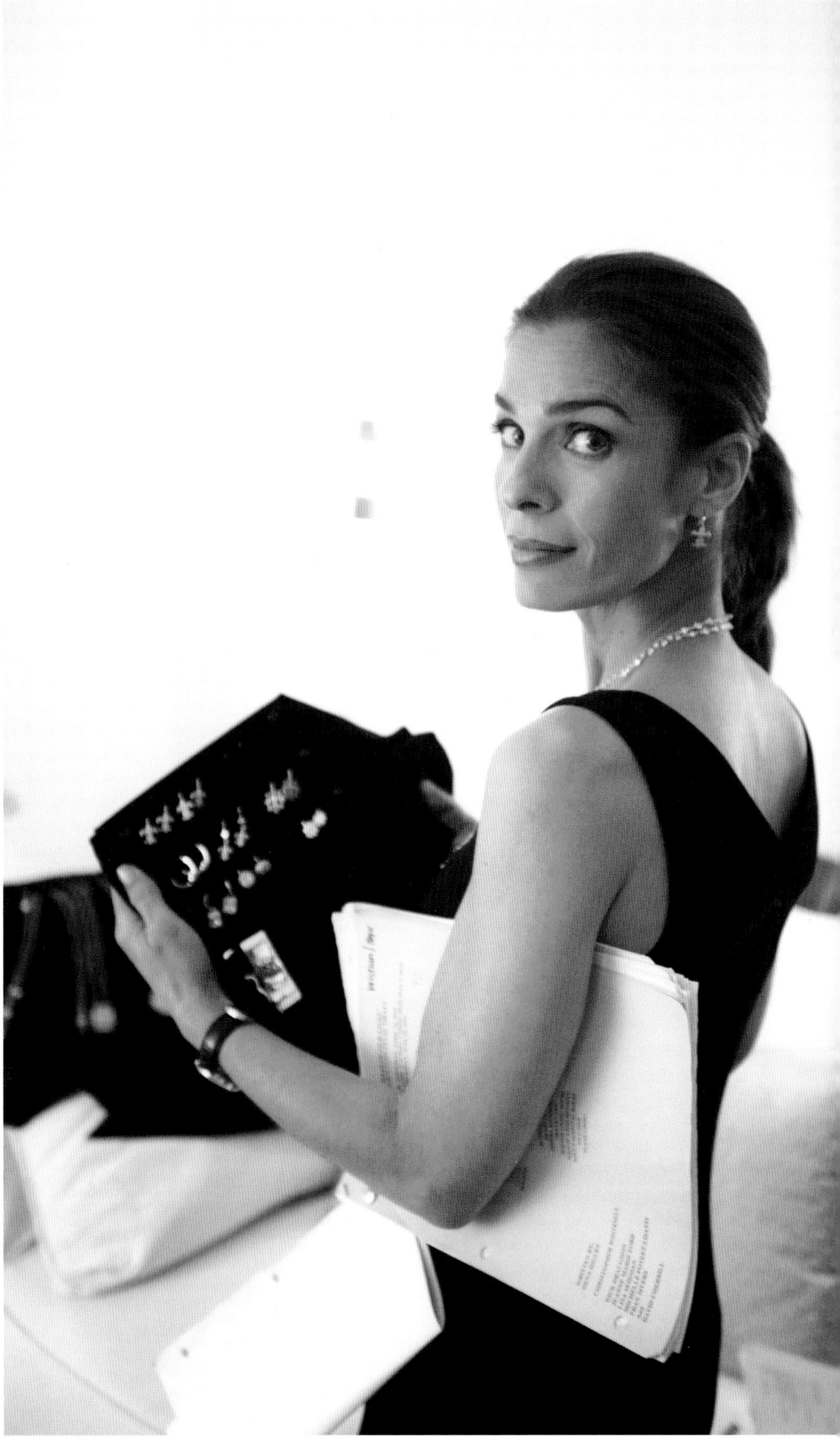

A RARE ON-SET MOMENT CAPTURED—THE BRADYS; "ROMAN"/JOSH TAYLOR, "KIMBERLY"/PATSY PEASE, "BO"/PETER RECKELL, AND
"KAYLA"/MARY BETH EVANS ON "BO/HOPE'S" LIVING ROOM SET

"KATE"/LAUREN KOSLOW IN HER DRESSING ROOM

SPECIALTY HAND PROPS
NOT FOR SET DRESSING

THE HORTON'S

HAND PROP
USE ONLY
SAMI & LUCAS

HAND PROP USE ONLY
JOHN & MARLENA

DO NOT EAT!

FAKE FOOD FOR PROP

GROCERY BAGS.

FAKE
FRUIT

FAKE BREAD

Days of our Lives

The Loft

Hand Props
Designated & Generic
Please do not use designated

BARON'S

SALEM
YELLOW PAGES

HORTON KITCHEN

#7

KATE ROBERTS
STORYLINE PROPS
PHILIP KIRIAKIS
KIRIAKIS FAMILY

ROMAN'S OFFICE
COFFEE SET-UP

KIRIAKIS TERRACE
BAR SET-UP

SALEM INN SUITE
BAR SET-UP

Happy Anniversary
Bo & Hope

Victor Kiriakis

HOPE'S

ABOVE:
EXECUTIVE PRODUCER/KEN CORDAY, HEAD WRITER/
DENA HIGLEY, CO-HEAD WRITER/CHRISTOPHER WHITESELL,
AND CO-EXECUTIVE PRODUCER/GARY TOMLIN AFTER A
SCRIPT MEETING

LEFT:
DIRECTOR/HERB STEIN

RIGHT:
DIRECTOR/PHIL SOGARD

PRIOR PAGE:
STAGE MANAGER/STUART HOWARD
SECURES PROPS WITH CAST

LAST-MINUTE INPUT FROM GARY TOMLIN TO "SHANE"/CHARLES SHAUGHNESSY AND "KIMBERLY"/PATSY PEASE AS STAGE ELECTRICIAN/TROY TURNER, WARDROBE HANDLER/ELIZABETH CASHMORE-FEENEY, AND BOOM OPERATOR/HARRY YOUNG CONTINUE WORKING

"JUSTIN"/WALLY KURTH
GETTING INTO CHARACTER

TEASER -

327

NIGHT

1326-VIII-A, NATHAN AND

NATHAN

e real disappointed if we

ut tonight?

STEPHANIE

ot.

NATHAN

I was just kind of looking forward to a

quiet night at home.

STEPHANIE

Sure. No, problem.

(STARTS OUT)

Call me tomorrow, okay?

NATHAN

Stephanie.

(SHE TURNS BACK)

I meant a quiet night at home. With

Chloe... you seem really upse

Is something wrong?

CHLOE

Yeah. You.

CARLY

Me.

CHLOE

nk I'm not good enough f

CARLY

not true!

CHLOE

)

shut your lying mouth!

CHARLIE	ROMAN
CHLOE	STEPHANIE
DANIEL	HOMELESS WOMAN U/5
DEALER	
DR. BAKER	EXTRAS:
GABI	BACK ROOM (2 Poker Players)
HOPE	BRADY PUB (3 Patrons + 1 Waitress)
MELANIE	NURSES' STATION (1 Doctor + 1 Nurse +
MOTEL CLERK	1 EMT)

SETS:
BACK ROOM
BRADY PUB/EXT.
DANIEL'S APARTMENT/CORI
HOPE'S KIRIAKIS BEDROOM/CO
KIRIAKIS MANSION/EXT.
MAGGIE'S KITCHEN/EXT.
NICE PIER
NURSES' STATION/BRADY'S HOSPIT
PARK
PHILIP/MELANIE'S BED LIMBO (RE
NATHAN'S BED LIMBO

WRITTEN BY:
DENA HIGLEY

CHRISTOPHER WHITESELL

RICK DRAUGHON
JEANNE MARIE FORD

CONTROL BOOTH: PRODUCER/MARY-KELLY WEIR, TECHNICAL DIRECTOR/MICHAEL CARUSO, DIRECTOR/ALBERT ALARR, ASSOCIATE DIRECTOR/MIKE FIAMINGO, PRODUCTION ASSOCIATE/KRISTA CREMIDAN, LIGHTING DIRECTOR/TEDDY POLMANSKI, AND AUDIO ENGINEER/ROGER CORTES

EDITOR/
LUGH POWERS

VIDEO ENGINEER/
ALEXIS HANSON

TOP: PRODUCER/NOEL MAXAM
BOTTOM: POST AUDIO MIXER/ZOLI OSAZE

"DANIEL"/SHAWN CHRISTIAN IN HIS DRESSING ROOM

"STEFANO"/JOE MASCOLO IN HIS DRESSING ROOM

...SO ARE THE DAYS OF OUR LIVES

PHOTOGRAPHY

CORDAY PRODUCTIONS/BRIAN LIPCHIK, 1, 56–253
(except as denoted below)

CORDAY PRODUCTIONS/JEFF VOORHEES, 74, 75, 124,
125, 126, 127, 128, 132, 133, 150, 151, 184, 185, 196,
197, 205, 220, 221, 222, 223, 232, 233, 242, 256

NBCU PHOTO BANK, 2, 3, 5–49, 133 (bottom left) (except
as denoted below; by page number)

NBCU PHOTO BANK/FRED SABINE, 8,9

NBCU PHOTO BANK/PAUL W. BAILEY, 10, 11

NBCU PHOTO BANK/RON TOM, 12, 15

NBCU PHOTO BANK/GARY NULL, 13, 14, 16, 21, 27
(top right), 36, 44, 45

NBCU PHOTO BANK/HERB BALL, 18

NBCU PHOTO BANK/FRANK CARROLL, 22, 24, 25, 27
(bottom left)

NBCU PHOTO BANK/JOSEPH DEL VALLE, 26 (bottom),
27 (bottom right), 32 (bottom), 33 (top)

NBCU PHOTO BANK/ALICE S. HALL, 27 (top left), 28

NBCU PHOTO BANK/CHRIS HASTON, 41

NBCU PHOTO BANK/WENDY PERL, 47 (top left)

NBCU PHOTO BANK/JEAN KRETTLER, 47 (top right)

CORDAY PRODUCTIONS/LESLIE BOHM, 23, 26 (top right), 29

PHOTOGRAPHS PROVIDED BY KEN BANK, 35 (upper right),
42, 43

CORDAY PRODUCTIONS/JEFF KATZ, 34 (upper right)

COURTESY OF JPI STUDIOS, 30, 31 (top right), 32 (bottom left),
32 (top), 33 (bottom), 37, 38, 39, 48 (top), 49, 50-51, 52 (photo
only), 54 (photo only), 55 (photo only), 104, 105, 110, 111,
134, 135, 158, 159, 160, 161, 202, 203, 222 (top) , 238, 239

Page 35 (bottom right) and page 40 © 2005 CPT Holdings, Inc.
All rights reserved. Photographs taken by Aaron Rapoport.

SKETCHES
RICHARD BLOORE, 52, 53, 54, 55

Special thanks to Sourcebooks, Peter Lynch, Anne Hartman, Ashley Haag, Klear PR, Laura Gallagher, Kyley Jolna, NBC, NBCU Photo Bank, Jennifer Hozer, Julie Gollins, JPI Studios, Ruby Montgomery, Sony, Barry Felsen, Susan Seaforth Hayes, Allison Wait, and Greg Economos.